ACC. No: 02586271

PARACHUTIST
AT FINE LEG
AND OTHER UNUSUAL
OCCURRENCES FROM

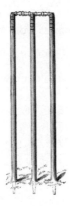

ALSO BY GIDEON HAIGH AND PUBLISHED BY AURUM

Ashes 2005

Many a Slip: A Diary of a Club Cricket Season

Mystery Spinner: The Life and Death of an
Extraordinary Cricketer

Peter the Lord's Cat and Other Unexpected
Obituaries from Wisden

Downed Under: The Ashes in Australia 2006-7

Silent Revolutions: Writings on Cricket History

PARACHUTIST
AT FINE LEG
AND OTHER UNUSUAL
OCCURRENCES FROM
WISDEN

EDITED BY

Gideon Haigh

First published 2007 by Aurum Press Limited
7 Greenland Street
London NW1 0ND
www.aurumpress.co.uk

by arrangement with John Wisden & Co.

Entries copyright © 2007 John Wisden & Co.
Introduction and selection copyright © Gideon Haigh 2007

The extracts in this book were first published in
Wisden Cricketers' Almanack.

Wisden and its woodcut device are registered trademarks
of John Wisden & Co Ltd.

All rights reserved. No part of this book may be reproduced or utilized
in any form or by any means, electronic or mechanical, including
photocopying, recording or by any information storage and retrieval
system, without permission in writing from Aurum Press Ltd.

A catalogue record for this book is available from the British Library.

ISBN-10 1 84513 256 4
ISBN-13 978 1 84513 256 9

1 3 5 7 9 10 8 6 4 2
2007 2009 2011 2010 2008

Designed by Peter Ward
Typeset in Adobe Jenson by M Rules
Printed and bound in Great Britain by MPG Books, Bodmin, Cornwall

Contents

INTRODUCTION

Cricket is a funny game, but partakes of its fun seriously. Only a game so traditional, so formal and so ritualised could find so much scope for the odd, the unexpected and the ridiculous. For 'unusual occurrences' to be noted, there must be a firmly understood sense of the usual. It is therefore, perhaps, not surprising to find such a wealth of the bizarre in the sporting world's most po-faced and pedantically exact pages: the 144 editions of *Wisden Cricketers' Almanack*.

Lately, with its Chronicle and its Index of Unusual Occurrences, Wisden has drawn attention to the quaint and the quirky concealed in its bulk. But it's a custom that stretches back to its earliest editions, when the almanack's compilers showed uncommon relish for contests like One Leg v One Arm, Bats v Broomsticks, and Sixteen of Sheffield v Sixteen of the Country Around Sheffield, in which the cumulative age of the participants was 2,036 years. Even when it snorted the snuff of Victorian respectability, *Wisden* did not cease its surveillance to what took place on the field. In reports of Oxford v Cambridge, Eton v Harrow and Canterbury Week during the nineteenth century, the cricket vies for importance and is sometimes decidedly secondary to the social whirl, whether it is the university fixture of June 1877 brought to a halt by slowly promenading society belles ('"Truly," said a 20-years' regular attendant at Lord's, "It is a sight that never had an equal on a cricket-ground"'), or the programme performed by the 'Old Stagers' during their theatrics at Canterbury four years later ('The Charming Woman', 'Out of Light', 'Tit for Tat', 'A Thumping Legacy' and 'Hester's Mystery').

Thus *Parachutist at Fine Leg*: a personal selection of episodes,

irruptions, vignettes, digressions, detours and more than a few deba-
cles, all reported in the classic *Wisden* vein. The title story pertains to
one Anthony Adams Jnr, a Chilean cricketer-cum-parachutist, who
combined his two great interests by arriving for a 2004 game with his
club La Dehesa from above, 'landing at fine leg, peeling off his gear and
taking his place in the field at the very spot where he landed'. The key
to this story which gives it the authentic *Wisden* stamp is not, I think,
the parachute, nor even Chile – it is the insistent exactitude of the
fielding position, fine leg.

Unusual occurrences in cricket might be divided between those
that are endogenous, occurring within the game, and those that are
exogenous, transpiring when there is some visitation from or reminder
of the world outside. The first category here is represented princi-
pally by extraordinary feats of batting, bowling, fielding and umpiring,
curious games, curious players and, a hardy perennial, instances of
ethical elasticity. *Wisden* had an eye and ear for this even in the days of
'Rule Britannia' and Henry Newbolt's 'Vitai Lampada', and wasn't
always as censorious as might be imagined. The brothers Grace, happy
enough to 'play the game' but keener on winning it, were especially
beloved. Abducting prospective teammates, appealing for everything
including hit-the-ball-twice, W. G. strides majestically through these
pages; there's also the superbly adamant E. M., telling an umpire who
had just called over: 'Shut up, I am going to have another'.

High dudgeon and high-handedness are complementary influ-
ences in this period. *Wisden* reported Derbyshire's John Hulme refusing
to take the field in June 1894 because of 'personal grievance against one
of the players' arising from some 'unpleasantness', Somerset's H. T.
Hewett retiring from a match at Scarborough in September 1895 after
'insulting remarks' from the crowd, Neville Cardus' tirelessly tactless
hero Archie MacLaren dogmatically ending a game because of a heel

print in the pitch, the quintessential English amateur C. B. Fry casu-
ally disdaining to return to a ground after rain he judged too heavy. In
a time of a firmer social hierarchies and a more tactful and deferential
press, players arguably got away with more than they do in these days
of referees, codes, omniscient television cameras and omnipotent
pundits.

In a technical sense, the unusual is not guaranteed to remain so.
One of this book's most illuminating historical curios is a report from
June 1896 of what sounds very like a reverse sweep: Yorkshire's John
Brown losing his wicket after scoring a century by 'foolishly hitting
back-handed at a lob'. The stroke is next glimpsed, very specifically,
sixty-nine years later, in a Single Wicket Competition, with Mushtaq
Mohammad changing 'in a flash from a right-handed batsman to a
left-handed player to deal with a ball pitched well outside what was
originally his off stump'. On the other hand, Bernard Anderson's 'overhead tennis smash' in 1934 and Dermot Reeve's hands-free exploits
against Hants in 1996 have attracted no notable adherents. And if
anyone parallels Mark Pettini's 27-ball hundred last season at Leicester
and the 77 conceded from an over by Bert Vance in 1989–90, it will
only be regrettable.

The range of exogenous variation in cricket, meanwhile, is embod-
ied chiefly in a catalogue of meteorological and other phenomena,
including the astounding season of ice cricket in the winter of 1878–9,
and the veritable menagerie of animals that have gambolled and frol-
icked across *Wisden*'s pages: sparrows, swallows, partridges, dogs, foxes,
rabbits, deer, elk, sheep, boar, bees, wasps and even a few indolent
snakes. Scope for the latter has increased since the almanack began to
survey off-piste cricket more devotedly: the elk popped up in Finland,
for instance, while the boar laid waste a ground in France. But a subtle
reminder of cricket's rural origins has long been threaded through

Wisden's pages, as well as borne on its cover since 1938 in Eric Ravilious's famous fir-fringed woodcut.

Even when the intrusions from the non-cricket realm are of the most momentous kind, moreover, *Wisden* has shown a wonderful capacity for deadpan non-surprise. Its reporting of matches in wartime – like those here disturbed by 'the Battle of Britain', 'the liberation of Europe', 'the flying bombs' and the 'prolonged wait for "all clear"' (which did not prevent a result) – is some of its most remarkable and resonant. When a public schools game was disturbed by the detonation of a V1 200 yards from Lord's in August 1944, for instance, *Wisden* was there, timing the interruption at 'little more than half a minute', and reporting that spectators 'showed their appreciation of the boys' pluck with hearty hand-claps'. The almanack has nodded to survivors of Ladysmith, victors at Alamein, commanders at Jutland and a host of crowned heads. There are hints here of the Cold War too, such as Eisenhower at a Test in Pakistan, and Harold Wilson at an impromptu 'Test' in Moscow, shadowed by a suspicious NKVD.

Then again, who needs war when one considers some of the exquisite tortures that have lain in wait for cricketers down the years? Here will be found batsmen dismissed by consecutive balls in different innings, the first ball of each innings, for a 'king pair' in hat-trick, for a pair inside an hour and a quarter and for a pair spanning a painful 54 balls; look out, too, for bowlers conceding 34 in their maiden first-class over, 38 in a six-ball over, 250 from a single hit, seeing a ball they bowled vanish in the back of a long-distance lorry, and feeling 9kg of their body weight vanish in a single day's play. Cricket, as they say, tests character – if, of course, it doesn't break it first.

In its own way, *Parachutist at Fine Leg* marks an unusual occurrence seldom recognised as such: the annual publication of *Wisden*. Who today would initiate a yearly book of 1,700 pages containing more than any sane person need know about the twelve months of cricket just past? Yet it lands each April with a thud of reassuring familiarity, to be pored over by the cognoscenti, and obsessed over by completists. One is not merely mentioned by *Wisden*; one is incorporated in it, never to escape. The A. S. I. Berry involved in the madcap idea of a 24-hour game of cricket of Parker's Piece in June 1973 has made the best of this, recently becoming the almanack's editor.

It is almost as though once one is incorporated by *Wisden*, one never escapes. In the age of abundant real-time information and a culture of instantaneous gratification, *Wisden*'s abiding popularity is deeply mysterious. It exists as a kind of statistical Stonehenge – a sentinel whose use by past generations is only dimly understood, but which somehow visibly incarnates cricket's continuity, autonomous within while also inseparable from the game it is dedicated to documenting. If cricket is a funny game, then *Wisden* is assuredly a funny book – albeit, of course, imbued with the deep seriousness of cricket itself.

Gideon Haigh

Extreme Batting

LANCASHIRE IN 1876

Lancashire batting in 1876 resulted in Mr Hornby being well ahead of the others in the three important average columns, he and Barlow scoring more runs than any other seven men. Both played up to their well-known form of brilliant hitting and rapid scoring by the one and stolid defence and slow scoring by the other; and perhaps their distinctively peculiar forms were never more aptly illustrated than when in Lancashire's first innings against Nottinghamshire, at Nottingham, the first wicket (Mr Hornby's) fell with the score as follows:

Mr A. N. Hornby c Selby b Oscroft	44
Barlow not out	0
B 1	1
	(1 wkt) 45

WILLIAM DRUMMOND HAMILTON
(1859–1914)

In 1882 he gained his blue at Oxford, but in the match with Cambridge (in which he was so nervous that he once started the wrong way when called for a run) scored only 9 and 0.

MR VERNON'S TEAM v EIGHTEEN OF WAGGA WAGGA
Wagga Wagga, February 28, 29, 1888

A single innings victory for the Englishmen, with five runs to spare. The order of going in was decided by drawing lots.

NOTTINGHAMSHIRE v YORKSHIRE
Nottingham, June 1, 2, 3, 1896

At this period of the season the Yorkshiremen were batting in wonderful form, and in scoring their 450, they showed some very brilliant cricket; Brown, who lost his wicket in foolishly hitting back-handed at a lob, taking the chief honours.

THE HIGHEST INDIVIDUAL SCORE ON RECORD
Clifton College – Clarke's v North Town

A junior house match at Clifton College, begun on Thursday, June 22, 1899, and completed on the following Wednesday, is noteworthy for having produced the greatest score known to have been made by a single player in a game of any description. The hero of the occasion, A. E. J. Collins, was batting for six hours and fifty minutes, his innings being continued in unequal instalments during five days. His hits included a 6, four 5s, thirty-one 4s, thirty-three 3s and 146 2s.

Clarke's

Collins not out	628
Champion c Monteath b Rendall	27
Gilbert b Crew	9
Sudely c Davis b Sainsbury	8
Sheriff b Crew	6
Galway b Crew	11
Whittey c and b Monteath	42
Spooner b Monteath	0
Leake b Monteath	32
Raine b Monteath	14
Redfern c Fuller-Eberle b Crew	13
Extras	46
	836

CHARLES PERCY McGAHEY
(1871–1935)

Mr Percy Perrin, the best batsman in England who never played Test cricket, and still well known as one of the present Selection Committee, gives this appreciation of his old colleague:

Charles McGahey, in my view, was one of the most popular and kindest-hearted players ever seen in first-class cricket; certainly he was most encouraging to any young player. I have known him on many occasions to go out of his way to give a youngster good advice. Dry humour was an outstanding feature of his attractive characteristics. Having played with him more or less for 25 years I consider McGahey one of the very best cricketers Essex ever had. Really a magnificent cricketer he was undoubtedly the hardest hitter I ever faced. The opposite batsman had to keep his eyes open, as McGahey used to jump to the ball and drive back very straight. On one occasion he drove the ball back so hard that he broke his partner's arm!

I well remember one instance of his quick thinking wit when I was in at the other end. McGahey was 99, he played at the next ball, said 'Come one' but failed in his stroke and was bowled. As he passed by on the way to the pavilion he said to the bowler, 'Lucky for you I wanted a drink.'

GREGOR MacGREGOR
(1869–1919)

D. L. A. Jephson writes: Silent, imperturbable as MacGregor usually was, occasionally his splendid keenness broke through his cold reserve. Surrey, as was often the case, were hard pressed by our old rivals Middlesex, and on the morning of the third day at The Oval, seemed certain to lose the match. There had been some rain and the wicket was slow and easy, and with all their side to bat, Middlesex required only 150 or so to win. At the interval they had made 120 odd for three. At lunch I noticed that several of the amateurs had not even changed, so certain were they of the runs. I whispered to MacGregor: 'Mac, I should like to make those fellows change.' And he smiled. After lunch, after forty-five minutes of a hot sun, a wonderful change came 'o'er the spirit of their dream.' Hayward and Lockwood and the sticky wicket caused a rapid search for garments—wicket after wicket fell and MacGregor arrived only to be run out by Turkey Rawlin in his first over! As he passed Rawlin in the middle of the pitch, seeing he had no earthly chance to get in—he shouted in a voice literally broken with emotion: 'Great Scott, Turkey, what *have* you done?'

WESTERN PROVINCE v GRIQUALAND WEST
Cape Town, December 17, 19, 1921

Griqualand West, 135 and 270 (W. V. Ling, 43 and 83, top scorer in each innings); Western Province, 203 and 204 for four (M. J. Commaille 98 not out). Commaille had another ball or two bowled to him after the winning hit was made, to let him complete his century, and his score was returned at 102 not out in some quarters. But it is difficult to justify this procedure, though a similar thing was done in the case of R. H. Bettington at Eastbourne last year, and the century was allowed to rank.

AUSTRALIA v ENGLAND
Sydney, December 2, 3, 5, 6, 7, 1932

In his highest Test innings against Australia Sutcliffe batted seven hours and a quarter, but he hit only thirteen 4's. He had one great piece of luck when he was 43, playing a ball on to his wicket without, however, removing the bails.

OXFORD UNIVERSITY v MINOR COUNTIES
Oxford, May 30, 31, June 1, 1934

When the batsmen were running a three for a hit by Farrimond, each umpire signalled 'one short' so reducing the value of the stroke to a single.

BERNARD GERARD WENSLEY ATKINSON
(1901–1966)

In 1934 for Middlesex against Surrey at Lord's, he hit a short-pitched ball from A. R. Gover for six with what was described as 'an overhead lawn tennis smash'.

MISCELLANY
[1936]

In a rain-ruined match at Nottingham, G. O. Allen (Middlesex) batted on each of three days for 6 not out. Actually his innings occupied half an hour.

GLAMORGAN v INDIA
Cardiff, June 8, 10, 11, 1946

Without much chance of a definite finish Glamorgan reversed their batting order when following-on, but their efforts to treat the crowd to some big hitting were baulked by the Indians, who almost pulled off unexpected victory. To Judge occurred the extraordinary experience of being out first ball to successive deliveries—bowled in each innings by Sarwate.

KENT v HAMPSHIRE
At Canterbury, August 4, 6, 7, 1956

Ridgway needed a 6 off the last ball from Gray but his intended big hit produced only a snick for two, though he twice lapped Allan between wickets in his eagerness for runs.

ENGLAND v WEST INDIES
Birmingham, May 30, 31, June 1, 3, 4, 1957

Pairaudeau occupied an abnormal amount of time in the middle for a man who scored only a single. He spent three and a quarter hours as runner for Walcott and then five hours for Worrell.

GLAMORGAN v NORTHAMPTONSHIRE
Swansea, June, 10, 11, 12, 1964

Norman, the Northamptonshire opening batsman, had the unenviable distinction of being dismissed with the first ball of each innings on Wednesday when twenty-three wickets went down.

SINGLE WICKET COMPETITION IN 1965

Mushtaq Mohammad showed batsmanship of the highest quality in winning the Charrington Single Wicket Competition played over two days at Lord's on July 15 and 16. Sent in by d'Oliveira in the final, the Pakistani, qualifying by residence for Northamptonshire, replied with 76 runs off the allotted eight overs, placing the ball delightfully wide of fieldsmen for most of his eleven 4's and over their heads for two 6's, one of which landed on the canopy above the Tavern. As a finale he changed in a flash from a right-handed batsman to a left-handed player to deal with a ball pitched well outside what was originally his off stump.

NOTTINGHAMSHIRE v LEICESTERSHIRE
Nottingham, August 18, 19, 20, 1965

Inman, the 29-year-old Leicestershire batsman from Colombo, established a world record on the final day by scoring 51 runs in eight minutes, 50 of these in two overs from Hill. Beginning his innings at 199 for three when Nottinghamshire were giving away cheap runs in the hope of a declaration, he took a single off the last ball of an over from Bolus and then hit 18 – 4, 4, 6, 4 – and 32 – 4, 6, 6, 6, 6, 4 – off successive overs from Hill. They were slow inviting deliveries which Inman pulled to, or over, the mid-wicket boundary. The previous record was by Jim Smith of Middlesex who scored fifty in eleven minutes against Gloucestershire at Bristol in 1938.

NOTES BY THE EDITOR, 1966
FARCE OF THE FASTEST FIFTY

A player from Ceylon, C. C. Inman, the Leicestershire left-hander, set up new world records for the fastest fifty which he completed in eight minutes with eleven scoring strokes against Nottinghamshire at Trent Bridge. This was another case of farcical third-day county cricket when the fielding side, through N. Hill, who served up slow full tosses, gave away runs to persuade the opposition to make a declaration that would provide a chance of a definite result. Not surprisingly, umpire J. S. Buller sent a report to MCC.

DERBYSHIRE v SURREY
Ilkeston, July 24, 25, 26, 1968

Derbyshire collapsed in startling fashion against the left-arm spin of Harman, whose eight for 16 included the hat-trick and was at the time the season's best bowling performance. Rhodes achieved a dubious distinction by being the hat-trick victim and collecting a 'King Pair'.

GLAMORGAN v NOTTINGHAMSHIRE
Swansea, August 31, September 1, 2, 1968

This was the history-making match in which the incredible Garfield Sobers created a new world record by hitting six 6s in a six-ball over. Somehow one sensed that something extraordinary was going to happen when Sobers sauntered to the wicket. With over 300 runs on the board for the loss of only five wickets, he had the right sort of platform from which to launch a spectacular assault, and the manner in which he immediately settled down to score at a fast rate was ominous.

Then came the history-making over by the 23-year-old Malcolm Nash. First crouched like a black panther eager to pounce, Sobers with lightning footwork got into position for a vicious straight drive or pull. As Tony Lewis, Glamorgan's captain, said afterwards, 'It was not sheer slogging through strength, but scientific hitting with every movement working in harmony.' Twice the ball was slashed out of the ground, and when the last six landed in the street outside it was not recovered until the next day. Then it was presented to Sobers and will have a permanent place in the Trent Bridge Cricket Museum.

HAMPSHIRE v MIDDLESEX
Portsmouth, July 19, 1970

Middlesex won by eight wickets. Parfitt's 'pocket computer' and a hard-hit 49 by Russell took Middlesex to victory in a rain-affected match. Parfitt's 'computer' – a piece of paper on which he had recorded Hampshire's over-by-over score – was vital for Middlesex. He knew his side not only had to score 135 in 35 overs to win, but they also had to keep ahead of the Hampshire total for each over in case rain ended play abruptly. In fact, they always kept ahead and would have won at any stage after ten overs. Middlesex found the men for the situation in Russell and Parfitt, both of whom paused to consult the 'computer' every other over.

24-HOUR MARATHON AT CAMBRIDGE

Something unique for cricket took place on June 14/15 1973 at Parker's Piece, Cambridge. At 5 p.m. on June 14 two sides comprised of members of the Cambridge University Cricket Society took the field and at 5 p.m. the following day the same 22 players left the field having played cricket continuously except for a 'lunch' break, to MCC Laws for 24 hours. As well as creating a new world record for continuous cricket the effort raised over £170 for charity.

Each side had five innings in the match and a total of 1,395 runs were scored off 367 overs. During the hours of darkness gas lights illuminated the playing area, and light coloured cricket balls, specially prepared by Alfred Reader, were used.

In the period of darkness between 1 a.m. and 4 a.m. Roger Coates scored the only century of the match. Though the light was adequate the captains, Peter Such and David Langley, agreed to suspend fast bowling during the night on the grounds of safety.

At the end of an extremely exhausting 'day's' play Roger Coates, in a small ceremony, was presented with the prize for the best batting performance, by a Haig representative, and Philip Cornes received a trophy from a representative of Alfred Reader for the best bowling performance. Scores:

Langley's XI: 59, 179, 83, 200, 161. Total 682 runs.

Such's XI: 126, 254/8 dec., 121, 142/8 dec, 70/3. Total 713 runs.

Teams: Langley's XI: T. Brown, A. Ave, R. Court, J. Brett, J. Chambers, D. J. Yeandle, T. Wald, J. Preston, N. Peace, M. Coultas, D. Langley.

Such's XI: R. Coates, P. Such, P. Cornes, A. Radford, M. Williams, A. S. I. Berry, J. Burnett, P. Kinns, M. Shaw, R. Henson, M. Furneaux.

WARWICKSHIRE v WORCESTERSHIRE
Birmingham, May 29, 31, June 1, 1976

Jones, a youngster from Shropshire, who had fielded brilliantly, held on for fifty minutes surrounded by fielders and actually played through 20 overs before scoring a run.

MCC v NOTTINGHAMSHIRE
Lord's, May 1, 3, 4, 1982

Todd had the unenviable distinction of making a 'king pair'. Newman dismissing him with the first ball in each of Nottinghamshire's innings.

WORCESTERSHIRE v CAMBRIDGE UNIVERSITY
Worcester, June 16, 18, 19, 1984

In the first innings, Garlick, the Cambridge seam bowler, achieved his first run after nine consecutive first-class innings without scoring.

AN UNUSUAL DOUBLE IN 1986

Phil Watson, of the NCI club in Cambridge, played for their first and second teams last year – on the same afternoon. The two teams were playing on adjoining pitches on Parker's Piece, Cambridge, which enabled Watson to open the batting for NCI's first team in a Senior League game against Cherry Hinton, and then, when he was out for 5 after fifteen overs, to field for the second team, who were one man short, in their Junior League match against Sotham. He later opened the batting for the second team and scored 46 in 25 overs before returning to field for the first team. Cambridgeshire Cricket Association said later that there appeared to be nothing in their rules to forbid such an occurrence but that this would be rectified. Not that NCI benefited from their itinerant cricketer. Both teams lost.

IRELAND v SCOTLAND
Coleraine, July 18, 19, 20, 1987

When Scotland batted again, Russell suffered the ignominy of a pair, despite facing 32 balls in the first innings and 22 in the second.

WORLD RECORD PARTNERSHIP

A world record partnership of 664 runs unbroken for the third wicket was compiled by two schoolboys during the Harris Shield tournament for Bombay schools. Vinod Kambli, a sixteen-year-old left-hander, and fourteen-year-old Sachin Tendulkar were playing for Sharadashram Vidyamandir (English) against St Xavier's High School at the Sassanian Ground (Azad Maidan) in Bombay on February 23, 24, 25, 1988. Kambli hit three sixes and 49 fours in his innings of 349 not out and followed it by taking six wickets for 37, bowling off-breaks, as St Xavier's were dismissed for 145, leaving Sharadashram Vidyamandir (English) the winners by 603 runs. Tendulkar's 326 not out contained one six and 48 fours.

GLAMORGAN v MIDDLESEX
Abergavenny, June 10, 12, 13, 1989

It was a splendid finish to a match which produced 1,221 runs – and the memory of the Glamorgan secretary wading into an adjacent brook to retrieve the ball after one of Shastri's sixes.

CRICKET IN NEW ZEALAND
[1989–90]

Unfortunately for Wellington, the season will be remembered for their farcical tactics at the end of the third day of their return match against

Canterbury. In order to narrow the 94-run gap between the two sides, in the hope of then buying the last two wickets to win the game, Wellington captain Erwin McSweeney incurred the wrath of cricket purists by instructing his bowlers to toss up a series of deliberate no-balls. In the penultimate over, comprising 22 balls, Robert Vance conceded a record 77 runs (14446464141166666600401), 69 coming from the bat of the Canterbury wicket-keeper, Lee Germon. In the circumstances the question of whether Germon's feat should go in the record books is debatable. As it turned out, McSweeney's tactics almost cost him the game, which ended in a draw with the scores level after the final over, bowled by Evan Gray, had produced a further 17 runs. The scoreboard attendants could not keep up with the rapid run-rate from the last two overs, and neither side realised how close Canterbury were to victory until the match was over.

THE LANCASHIRE LEAGUES
[1990]

The fastest scoring of the season came from Stockport's Australian professional, Steve Wundke, who hit the Rochdale spinner, Neil Avery, for five consecutive sixes and completed his fifty in twelve balls.

PAKISTAN v SRI LANKA
Singapore, April 2, 1996

When Aamir Sohail asked Sri Lanka to bat in the second attempt at starting the game, Jayasuriya exploded into action with the quickest century in the history of limited-overs internationals. He rushed from a 32-ball 50 to a 48-ball hundred, with seven sixes and nine fours, easily beating Mohammad Azharuddin's 62 balls against New Zealand in 1988-89. Three balls later, he overtook Gordon Greenidge's record of eight sixes in a one-day international, set against India the same season. He had hit four successive sixes off Sohail in the most expensive over ever bowled at this level: it yielded 30 runs, 29 to Jayasuriya and one wide. Jayasuriya was eventually out for 134, out of 196 for two, from 65 balls, with 11 sixes and 11 fours (in fact, his last scoring stroke came off his 58th ball, before a final lull).

WARWICKSHIRE v HAMPSHIRE
Birmingham, May 16, 17, 18, 20, 1996

Hampshire's triumph was overshadowed, however, by the controversy surrounding Reeve's batting tactics on the final afternoon. He decided to counter Maru's left-arm spin from over the wicket by throwing his bat away, to avoid being caught off lifting deliveries. Reeve did this 15 times as he scored 22 from 89 balls, and argued that it was within the Laws. But MCC later ruled that an umpire could 'seriously consider' giving a batsman out for obstruction in these circumstances, because the action is likely to impede the close catchers.

BANGOR GRAMMAR SCHOOL IN 1997

In the seven-wicket win at King's, Macclesfield, a ball hit out of the ground bounced on to a lorry, last seen heading towards Alderley Edge.

HAMPSHIRE v SRI LANKANS
Southampton, August 22, 23, 24, 1998

Sri Lankan Arnold was out twice for nought in 75 minutes, both times to Morris, facing a total of nine balls.

RECORD FOR CLAYTON

Jon Clayton will enter cricket record books after hitting 38 runs from one over during the 1997–98 Country Carnival. Clayton, playing for South East, struck six sixes and a two from an over off Murray Districts medium-pacer Darren Nitschke. The sequence was as follows 6666266, the sixth delivery being a no-ball. Clayton, who was eventually dismissed for 80, said: 'Apart from the fifth ball, all the others were in the right spot so I thought I'd have a go. It was all pre-meditated.'

LEICESTERSHIRE v ESSEX
Leicester, September 20, 21, 22, 23, 2006

Essex were desperate for a win to ensure promotion, and Leicestershire, with nothing at stake, were content to play along. The upshot was one of the maddest half-hours in cricket history. Robinson and Nixon donated 186 runs in 9.4 overs to set up a declaration. Along the way, after more than 49,000 centuries in the history of first-class cricket, Mark Pettini became the first man to score one entirely in boundaries: 114 not out with 12 fours, 11 sixes and six dot balls. All the runs, except for one four, came off Robinson's dollies, lobbed in from a couple of paces. His hundred came in 24 minutes and 27 balls and, absurd though it was, it achieved its first objective. Essex were able to declare and set a target of 301 in 73 overs. But there was no happy ending for them.

Hit Records

OXFORD CIRCUIT v MIDLAND CIRCUIT
Lord's, June 23, 1875

In Mr Atkinson's 31 were a square-leg hit out of the ground for 6 past the grand stand, and an on-drive into the corner below the pavilion, for which 9 runs were made before the ball was returned.

AN INNINGS OF 403 RUNS – 170 RUNS IN 65 MINUTES
'A Clean Drive for 10'

The match wherein all this occurred was RE's v RMA, at Woolwich, last August 1873. The 403 runs were made by the RE Eleven, the 170 runs in sixty-five minutes were hit by Mr Renny-Tailyour and Mr H. W. Smith (RE's), and it was Mr H. W. Smith who made 'the clean drive for 10'. (Mr Tailyour made 137; Mr Smith, 100.)

2nd LIEUT. HAROLD J. GOODWIN
(1886–1917)

On June 1 and 8 in a House match at Marlborough, he scored 365 for Cotton House v Littlefield, making 276 for the first wicket with G. V. Sturgeon (73), and adding 264 for the second with M. P. Thorburn (83). He 'sent the 200 up with a hit for eleven'!!

GEORGE GILBERT
(1829–1906)

At The Oval, in 1851, he played a single-wicket match against Mr F. P. Miller, the Surrey captain, in which a curious occurrence took place. The latter cut a ball which went round the boundary stump. Gilbert threw the ball at the wicket but, as it did not pass within bounds, was told to fetch it back and try again. During the argument Mr Miller ran 13 for the hit.

GEORGE EDWARD HEMINGWAY
(1872–1907)

On one occasion, when playing a single-wicket match against his two brothers, he hit the ball into a bed of nettles; the fieldsmen quarrelled as to who should recover it, and during the argument the batsman ran about 250.

MCC AND GROUND v HUNTINGDONSHIRE
Lord's, July 31 and August 1, 1871

From 174 Hearne and West increased the score to 235 and the Club's innings ended for 247, Hearne having made 108 by a leg-hit to the bat stacks for 6 (lost ball cried when 5 had been run), a 5, four 4s, etc.

MIDDLESEX v GLOUCESTERSHIRE
Lord's, June 13, 14, 1881

Mr Vernon's next important hit was off Woof, through the open door of the Tennis Court, and as a light had to be obtained to find the ball, 'lost ball' was called and 6 scored.

Clothing and Equipment

THE FIRST ELEVEN OF MCC AND GROUND v
THE NEXT TWENTY
Lord's, May 9, 1872

This was an experimental match, wherein wickets were used one inch higher, one inch wider, and somewhat thicker than the orthodox 27 by eight. Rylott was the only bowler who hit the big (and ugly) wickets in the Eleven's innings, but Alfred Shaw bowled eight of 'The next Twenty'.

FROM DOCTOR GRACE TO PETER MAY
[1958]

Herbert Strudwick writes: I was naturally delighted when I got my first game with Surrey's first team, against the West Indies in 1900, though I had the feeling that a better man in Fred Stedman was standing down. Wicket-keepers used to have to put up with a good deal of knocking about then, for it was not always possible to gauge how the ball would come to you and our equipment was not what it is now. Stedman used to protect his chest with a copy of the South Western Railway time-table and on one occasion, after receiving a specially heavy blow, he remarked to a team-mate: 'I shall have to catch a later train tonight. That one knocked off the 7.30!'

SURREY v LONDON COUNTY
The Oval, April 13, 14, 15, 1903

In accordance with a recently-issued regulation of the Marylebone Club, the umpires tested the width of the bats with gauges, and more than one player had to get his bat shaved.

H. O. ('BLUM') BLOOMFIELD
(1891–1973)

A noted London club batsman. He wore spectacles and plimsolls when batting.

SOMERSET v SUSSEX
Taunton, May 21, 22, 1919

On the second afternoon Sussex, with the score at a tie, had a wicket to fall, the remaining batsman being Heygate who was crippled by rheumatism. It was understood when the innings began that he would not be able to bat and as there was some doubt as to whether he would come in, one of the Somerset players – not J. C. White, the acting captain – appealed to Street, the umpire, on the ground that the limit of two minutes had been exceeded. Street pulled up the stumps and the match was officially recorded as a tie.

THE HEYGATE INCIDENT

H. J. Heygate, the number eleven, was suffering from rheumatism and the effects of a war wound. He had not fielded and was not expected to bat. Indeed, he had not changed, wickets having gone down so suddenly, but wearing a blue lounge suit he limped out to bat. There was a friendly consultation between the captains, H. L. Wilson and J. C. White, but so slow had been his progress that the umpires, A. E. Street and F. G. Roberts, decided he had exceeded his two minutes and pulled up the stumps, declaring the result a tie. This decision was upheld by MCC after widespread comment on the most controversial situation which had occurred since Taunton became a cricket centre.

TEST MATCH CONTRETEMPS

Arthur Gilligan writes: I recall that, in the second Test match between England and Australia at Melbourne in 1925, after only 15 runs were on the board – I was bowling at the time – I noticed that a great piece of leather had come off the ball. I immediately showed the ball to Umpire Bob Crockett, who consulted his colleague and a brand new ball was brought out.

Before lunch that day we had no fewer than four new balls with the total no more than 87! When we adjourned, we discovered that, by mistake, a wrong packet of balls had been delivered to the ground and that we had No. 3 grade cricket balls instead of No. 1. It was agreed between 'Herby' Collins and myself to play out the first innings with both sides using the No. 3 grade variety, and it is interesting now to record that we used eight new balls before the score reached 200 and Australia had seven.

I do not think that any similar incident can be brought to mind of the ball being changed so frequently in a Test or any other match. It came as quite a relief when we embarked upon the second innings.

HENRY ('HARRY') BAGSHAW
(1861-1927)
He was buried in his umpire's coat and with a cricket ball in his hand.

GLOUCESTERSHIRE v RAF
Gloucester, July 24, 1943
Sgt V. D. Guthrie of the Australian Air Force, who bowled for Gloucestershire but was not included in their batting order, wore an England football shirt borrowed from S. Barkas, the former England international, an instructor at his station.

ENGLAND v WEST INDIES
Port of Spain, February 11, 12, 13, 14, 16, 1948
Wearing a chocolate-coloured felt hat and chewing gum the whole time, Carew, in an unorthodox display, used the hook and pull freely in a dazzling exhibition.

SIR KENNETH WADE PARKINSON
(1908–1981)
A useful opening batsman, he played an innings once for the Free Foresters in which he faced five balls, all against the fast bowling of Philip Utley: the first sped to the boundary and was signalled four runs, the fifth bowled him. In the dressing-room afterwards, four large dents were to be seen in his tin leg.

GLOUCESTERSHIRE v YORKSHIRE
Bristol, June 21, 22, 23, 1961

The last day's play consisted of one ball. All the players changed into flannels for the rather farcical closing stage. Bainbridge bowled the one delivery needed and Bernard, whose name had been drawn out of a hat to accompany Nicholls to the wicket, off-drove it to the boundary.

HAMPSHIRE v GLOUCESTERSHIRE
Portsmouth, July 26, 27, 28, 1989

There was little further joy for the Gloucestershire bowlers as next day Smith ground out his first Championship century of the summer. On Smith's dismissal, Nicholas borrowed his bat and off 139 balls struck his third hundred in five innings, hitting sixteen fours in his 101.

SRI LANKA v AUSTRALIA
Colombo, September 5, 1992

The home team, in uniforms of faded turquoise with a white chest band, failed to build on a splendid foundation of 101 for the second wicket, laid by Hathurusinghe and Gurusinha, after Mahanama had fallen first ball. The Australians – who wore a rich salmon strip with a broad grey band and called themselves the 'Pink Panthers' – began uncertainly, and were 58 for three in the 18th over.

CRICKET IN HUNGARY
[1993]

In May, the *Hungarian Times* reported the formation of the Magyar Cricket Club, which intended to play three other teams of expatriates, with kit provided by the British Embassy, on a matting wicket at Obudai Island. Two months later, however, it was reported that the kit had been stolen.

ZIMBABWE v SOUTH AFRICA
Harare, October 22, 1995

de Villiers opened what became the final over by bowling a paper cup.

LANCASHIRE v YORKSHIRE
Manchester, August 13, 1996

Immediately the game was over, Bevan flew by helicopter to Heathrow to return to Australia, where his team-mates were preparing to tour Sri Lanka. Despite his disappointment, he could look back on one moment of light relief, when a ball he struck flew into two pieces; its leather cover, ripped by a fielder's boot, fell off as he hit it, prompting speculation about what might have happened had either section been caught.

SRI LANKA v ZIMBABWE
Colombo, September 3, 1996

Play was delayed eight minutes while the umpires hunted for the bails, which turned up in a groundsman's pocket.

PAKISTAN v NEW ZEALAND
Rawalpindi, November 28, 29, 30, December 1, 1996

The Test occupied only 258.4 overs, though the opening day saw several hold-ups. One was caused by sunlight dazzling the batsmen after tea, another, more conventionally, by bad light, but the oddest occurred at the start, when play was delayed 20 minutes because the Pakistan Cricket Board had forgotten to supply balls. The match eventually got under way using a ball bought from a local sports shop.

WELLINGTON v NORTHERN DISTRICTS
Wellington, February 23, 24, 25, 26 2001

Wellington secured the Shell Trophy on gaining a first-innings lead just before lunch on the third day. Yovich bowled the first ball after the break with a red apple, an event recorded on the official scoresheet.

GLAMORGAN v HAMPSHIRE
Cardiff, September 15, 16, 17, 18, 2005

Knowing the declaration was due one ball later, McLean arrived at the non-striker's end without gloves or pads; the umpires were not amused.

NORTHAMPTONSHIRE v SOMERSET
Northampton, May 3, 4, 5, 2006

Klusener (wearing a shirt proclaiming him as G. White, owing to a kit mix-up) pummelled a short boundary towards the West Stand, and his 147 on home debut gave him 335 for once out. White made his debut two games after his shirt.

LANCASHIRE v YORKSHIRE
Manchester, August 8, 9, 10, 11, 2006

Loye summed up the futility of the closing stages by fielding the final over in a black trilby lent by a spectator.

Weather Or Not

NOTTINGHAMSHIRE v SURREY
Nottingham, July 11, 12, 1872

The light was bad and gradually grew worse, a storm evidently brewing all round, but they played on until the score reached 180 runs; then (3.30) play was stopped by one of the most terrific outbursts of lightning, thunder, hail, rain and wind witnessed for many years in the Midlands. One account stated: 'In two minutes after the storm commenced every tent but the Printers' was blown down, the water lay in pools all over the ground, the flag pole was broken in twain, and many trees were dismantled.' Another account recorded: 'That four tents were blown down, the trees struck with lightning, and a greater portion of the ground submerged in water . . . The storm was truly alarming, and will make this match a remarkable event in cricket annals.'

A third local account thought it: 'The most violent storm ever witnessed in the district. To say it rained would be ridiculous; it poured in torrents, and not only flooded the ground, but, with the assistance of the wind and lightning, tore down the refreshment and ladies' booths as though they were mere shreds of paper.' Of course there was no more play on the stormy Friday, and as rain set in again at 11 a.m. on the Saturday and continued to fall until one o'clock 'the match was quashed'.

GENTLEMEN v PLAYERS OF ENGLAND
Prince's, July 5, 6, 7, 1877

The weather during the match was something frightful. A dull, murky, mucky afternoon on the first day culminated at evening in 'the storm of the season', when the lightning blazed, the air thundered, and the clouds poured out their waters in grand and awful form; and for one hour and a half London was drenched by the most furious rainstorm that fell over the big city in 1877. And who present at Prince's on the afternoon of the second day will readily forget that fierce outlet of lightning, thunder, rain, and hail that raged o'er the ground from 2.30 until 3, so thickly topping the turf with pea-sized hailstones as to give it the appearance of being coated with hoar-frost.

THE AUSTRALIANS v THE GENTLEMEN OF ENGLAND
Prince's, June 17, 18, 1878
Rain fell as A. Bannerman walked to the wickets, and the hundreds of upraised opened umbrellas around the ground was not only a curious sight, but those put up in front of the little press hut shut out all view of the play from the reporters, and all that could thenceforth be noted was that at a few minutes past four the Australians' innings closed for 75 runs, made from 103 overs, only one of the Eleven having been bowled.

SURREY v GENTLEMEN OF ENGLAND
The Oval, April 20, 21, 22, 1908
Early on Monday morning The Oval was covered with snow.

LEICESTERSHIRE v HAMPSHIRE
Leicester, August 16, 17, 18, 1933
Clouds of dust caused much discomfort to the batsmen, and the game was frequently interrupted owing to the bails falling off the stumps. After tea, much time having been wasted in trying to keep the bails in position, the umpires agreed to do without them. Consequently when the ball appeared to touch the stumps both Dawson and Shipman got the benefit of the doubt. Dawson, however, obviously playing on, a united appeal was upheld.

LANCASHIRE v HAMPSHIRE
Manchester, June 20, 21, 22, 1934
During most of the last day the wind was so troublesome that bails were dispensed with for long periods. Between the innings on the first day the motor roller broke down and had to be hauled away from the

middle of the ground. Also a sight-screen was blown down and broken so that the match was notable for several unusual occurrences.

BUCCANEERS v BRITISH EMPIRE XI
Lord's, August 31, 1940

'The Battle of Britain' interfered with the match, causing late arrivals, which necessitated an altered batting order and bringing about an early cessation when the Buccaneers seemed within sight of victory.

WEST OF ENGLAND v LORD'S XI
Lord's, July 8, 1944

For their first appearance at Lord's West of England were originally matched against A.A. Command, but, owing to the gunners being engaged with the flying-bombs, the opposition was changed to a Lord's XI.

A LORD'S XI v CANADA
Lord's, July 20, 1944

Americans were to have appeared at Lord's on this date, but their team, chosen entirely from bomber crews, were too busily engaged in the initial stages of the liberation of Europe campaign. Consequently Canada found themselves against stronger opposition.

AUSTRALIA v ENGLAND
Brisbane, November 29, 30, December 2, 3, 4 1946

Bad light and showers caused many stoppages, and the day ended with England 21 for one wicket. Late that evening a violent thunderstorm broke, and next day, when cricket was resumed after a delay of only ten minutes, England on a nightmare pitch took their score to 117 for five wickets before another thunderstorm flooded the ground. During this shortened day's play of three hours England fought valiantly. Lindwall, Miller and even Toshack made the ball lift alarmingly. Washbrook soon left, but Compton batted bravely; Edrich was struck repeatedly, and when Hammond came in nearly every ball from Lindwall rose head high. When taken at first slip immediately after lunch, Edrich had withstood the bowling for one and three-quarter hours. He scored only 16, but his was one of the most skilful batting displays I have ever seen. With Ikin going cheaply, half the side were out for 56. The bowling became even more difficult with the Australians pitching a better length, but Hammond, at his best, and Yardley raised the score to 117 without further loss when, following several appeals against the light, the players left the field. Then came the second storm, with hailstones as big as golf balls.

Contrary to expectations, the ground made a remarkable recovery next day in the brilliant sunshine, but the pitch proved more treacherous than ever, and, though England never gave up the unequal struggle, fifteen wickets fell in three and a half hours.

MCC TEAM v CEYLON
Colombo, October 1, 1950

As the players left the field at the end of the game flames sprang from a 100-yard-long bamboo-constructed stand. This had happened in some previous big matches at the Colombo Stadium and the Fire Brigade were ready. The outbreak was soon checked, but not before nearly half the coconut-matting roof had blazed.

ENGLAND v AUSTRALIA
Manchester, July 26, 27, 28, 30, 31, 1956

Conditions were terrible for cricket, a fierce wind making batting and bowling extremely difficult. Lignum bails were used and were most successful, not once being blown off.

TASMANIA COMBINED XI v SOUTH AFRICANS
Hobart, December 26, 27, 28, 1963

On the first day occurred a 20-minute hold up because of a gale – a stoppage believed to be unprecedented in Australian history – and a fine century by Potter. Potter alone defied the South African attack, and the gale, and his century included eleven 4s and one 6.

ENGLAND v WEST INDIES
Lord's, August 23, 24, 25, 27, 1973

This match will assuredly be known in cricket history as 'The Bomb Scare Test'. There was drama on the Saturday afternoon when 28,000 people were ordered to leave the ground following a telephone warning that a bomb had been planted. The call proved to be a hoax but no chances could be taken with the safety of players and spectators because an IRA bomb campaign was in full swing in London at the time.

The incident caused the loss of eighty-five minutes playing time and it was agreed that half an hour would be added to the day's play and further extra time provided for on Monday and Tuesday. But the triumphant West Indies had no need of it and they won with a day a half to spare. They swept aside a demoralized England side whose margin of defeat had been exceeded once only at Brisbane on the 1946–47 tour of Australia.

Half an hour after the interval, as Willis came out to join Arnold, the secretary of MCC announced over the loudspeakers that the ground would have to be cleared. For some time the players stayed in the middle surrounded by curious spectators. Eventually the West Indies went back to their hotel in Maida Vale and the England players to a tent behind the pavilion while police searched the empty stands. Thousands stayed on the playing area, refusing to leave.

When play resumed at 4.30 only a few thousand spectators had failed to return to watch cricket in an unreal atmosphere.

ESSEX v AUSTRALIANS
Chelmsford, July 6, 7, 8, 9, 1985

On the second day, play was interrupted for twenty minutes by a bomb scare, the crowd moving on to the playing area while the police searched the pavilion and stands.

CANCELLED TOUR

Suspicions that sabotage was the cause of the crash of an Air India plane off Ireland in June 1985, with the loss of over 300 lives, prompted an Indian team, led by S. M. Gavaskar, to cancel a proposed tour of Canada. The ill-fated aircraft had been on a flight from Canada to India.

AUSTRALIA v NEW ZEALAND
Brisbane, January 17, 1989

Quick thinking by the 'Gabba's curator, Kevin Mitchell, saved the match from being a washout. With New Zealand 137 for three after 40.3 overs, and Jones dominating the innings, Mitchell ran on to the pitch, his groundstaff and tractor following, and removed the stumps to the astonishment of umpires Crafter and Johnson. Within seconds a rain squall hit the ground, but the covers were on and the pitch was saved from becoming a quagmire. The curator's intervention meant that only 37 minutes of play were lost, although the match was reduced to 44 overs a side.

WEST ZONE v NEW ZEALANDERS
Rajkot, November 1, 2, 3, 1988

The match started three hours late because the tour manager, Mr Ken Deas, had sent the team's baggage by road from Bombay, and that took a while longer than anticipated.

AUSTRALIA v SRI LANKA
Perth, December 30, 1989

Two overs were lost at the start because the groundstaff had forgotten to mark the fielding circles, and later there was a disquieting delay while Channel Nine TV technicians repaired a sound-effects microphone in a stump. After their efforts, the stump stood taller than the rest, with the result that a replacement had to be found. The crowd did not appreciate the delay.

SRI LANKA v AUSTRALIA
Moratuwa, September 8-13, 1992

Matthews, with his fifth consecutive half-century of the series, and the dependable Healy eased any embarrassment after the loss of yet more time – three and a quarter hours – to rain on the final day. One joker added an extra touch to the statue of St Joseph positioned near the pavilion, supposedly to ward off foul weather: an umbrella.

CRICKET GROUNDS IN 1993

A high percentage of the games at Pontypridd have been ruined by rain. 'On a nice day it's a very attractive setting for cricket,' said a local official. 'Unfortunately, no one can remember a nice day.'

WORCESTERSHIRE v OXFORD UNIVERSITY
Worcester, June 17, 18, 19, 1994

Worcestershire might have won in two days after routing Oxford for 95, 245 behind. But county officials, anxious to salvage a Father's Day barbecue scheduled for the third day's lunch interval, persuaded acting-captain Illingworth not to enforce the follow-on.

TRANSVAAL v WESTERN PROVINCE
Johannesburg, January 27, 28, 29, 30, 1995

Lightning stopped play after a bolt hit close to the stadium, causing players to dive to the ground during E. O. Simons's run-up.

BORDER v BOLAND
Paarl, February 3, 4, 5, 6, 1995

It was reported that fried calamari stopped play when Cullinan hit a six off R. Telemachus into a frying pan. It was about ten minutes before the ball was cool enough for the umpires to remove the grease. Even then, Telemachus was unable to grip the ball and it had to be replaced.

WESTERN AUSTRALIA v TASMANIA
Perth, March 8, 9, 10, 11, 1996

Ridgway lost nine kilograms in the heat of the first day.

CRICKET IN BRUNEI DARUSSALAM
[1998]

When the players of Brunei and Sarawak trudged off the field on November 8, 1998, a 36-week cricket season came to an end. It had been interrupted just after it started, for health reasons. The longest drought in living memory led to major bush and scrub fires. As air quality deteriorated, the authorities issued warnings about engaging in outside physical activity, and when one fit young batsman was forced to retire ill, it was time to call a halt.

NEW ZEALAND WOMEN v ENGLAND WOMEN
Napier, February 22, 2000

The match went ahead as a day/night fixture despite one of the five banks of floodlights being stolen beforehand.

SUSSEX v LANCASHIRE
Hove, August 7, 2000

Some batsmen found the bungee jumping, situated behind the sightscreen, a distraction.

KENT v YORKSHIRE
Canterbury, May 19, 2002

Yorkshire's reply was delayed by a Gurkha pipe band, who disregarded the end of the interval and continued marching at long-on, oblivious to the bewildered players and umpires.

SURREY v KENT
The Oval, June 12, 13, 14, 2002

As play should have been resuming on the second day, Kent had two players at The Oval and ten stuck in traffic: a burst water main in Buckingham Palace Road, roadworks and an accident had conspired to cause gridlock. The umpires spoke to Alan Fordham, the ECB cricket operations manager, and decided to delay the start and make up lost time later. Play began 90 minutes late, with Kent forced to field a 12th man until 1.30, when Patel, whose BMW had overheated, finally arrived.

SURREY II v DERBYSHIRE II
The Oval, August 13, 14, 15, 2003

This historic match will be remembered for broken records and a bizarre stoppage. After Derbyshire declared their first innings on 580 for seven, Surrey openers Scott Newman and Nadeem Shahid hammered their way past 500, in 74 overs. At this point, New Zealand Test umpire Billy Bowden, renowned for the originality of his hand signals, added to his aura of eccentricity by producing a camera. He halted play to snap the grinning batsmen in front of the scoreboard, which showed 501 for nought. Bowden, getting his eye in before standing in the Fourth Test, took more photos at the close of play, by which time 547 had been plundered in just over two sessions. His sense of occasion was justified: the partnership of 552 was the best in the history of the Second XI Championship: Newman finally made 284 off 292 balls, with three sixes and 49 fours, Shahid 266 from 271 balls, with three sixes and 41 fours. After waiting padded-up for nearly a day, Surrey's No. 3, Christopher Murtagh, made one.

HOLLAND v WARWICKSHIRE
Rotterdam, May 3, 4, 2005

Warwickshire had far more trouble than anticipated: the ground was so new it did not show on the coach driver's satnav system. He drove the players to the old VOC Club, three miles away and now derelict, and they had to wander through the woods in the rain before they were rescued. At the ground, the tent in which they were sheltering was blown from its moorings by the wind.

Flora and Fauna

MCC AND GROUND v NOTTINGHAMSHIRE
Lord's, June 14, 15 1875

Wind and weather alone considered, this was the most *un*-enjoyable match ever played out at Lord's, for throughout those two days the wind blew big and bitter blasts from the W.S.W., so cold that the air was more fitting for Ulsters and mid-winter than summer suits and midsummer, and so strong that – in addition to other casualties – the wind broke clean in half the trunk of a full-sized sturdy elm tree that stood at that end of the Regent's Park nearest to Lord's Ground.

GEORGE PARR
(1826–1891)

He lived all his life in his native village, and the attendance at his funeral there showed the respect in which he was held. With the wreaths on his coffin was placed a branch from the tree at the Trent Bridge ground which has for a generation past been known as 'George Parr's Tree'. This name it acquired in connection with the great batsman's leg-hitting.

WILLIAM JUSTICE FORD
(1853–1904)

His longest measured hit was 143 yards 2 feet. He hit out of almost all the grounds upon which he played, including Lord's and the Aigburth ground at Liverpool. Playing once for MCC and Ground v Eastbourne, at the Saffrons, he hit J. Bray over the trees, the ball pitching 60 yards beyond them. On another occasion, when playing at Torquay, he hit a ball out of the ground (above the ordinary size), across a road, and so far into another field that it put up a brace of partridges.

MISCELLANY
[1936]

A sparrow was killed by a ball bowled by Jahangir Khan in the MCC and Cambridge University match at Lord's. T. N. Pearce, the batsman, managed to play the ball and the bird fell against the stumps without dislodging the bails. The bird is preserved as a relic in the pavilion at Lord's.

A CENTURY IN THE FIJI ISLANDS

Philip Snow writes: When I left Fiji in 1952, New Zealand was pressing for a repetition of the 1948 tour. Fijians, supreme guerrilla fighters volunteering for the Malayan campaign, including Petero Kumbunavanua, reserve wicket-keeper in my 1948 New Zealand touring team. Selected with two other Fijians and Ratu Sir Edward Thakombau to play for Negri Sembilan State against Perak in 1952, Petero added to cricket's rare ornithological connection. Fielding at square leg and disturbed by swallows swooping on flies, he snatched one from the air and put it in his *sulu* pocket.

BUT NOT A DUCK IN SIGHT

During the John Player League match between Warwickshire and Kent at Edgbaston on June 6, 1982 a fox – a stray Leicestershire supporter perhaps – ran around the ground behind the arm of the bowler, Derek Underwood, before disappearing into the crowd.

A week later, at The Oval where Surrey were playing Gloucestershire, a pigeon crept up behind the Surrey batsman Monte Lynch into the closest of short-leg positions, causing him to move away from the crease just as the bowler was about to deliver the ball.

As has happened with animals of the human variety, word of these invasions of the field of play spread quickly around the kingdom. At Trent Bridge in August, a rabbit ran on to the pitch, where it was apprehended by the Derbyshire captain Barry Wood.

ZIMBABWE v ENGLAND A
Harare, March 20, 21, 22, 1990

The final act was enlivened by Briant, who reached a confident hundred from 136 balls before the game was given up. Earlier, play had been briefly interrupted when a swarm of bees flew over the cricketers' heads, causing everyone to lie flat on the ground.

SURREY v YORKSHIRE
The Oval, September 16, 17, 18, 20, 1993

The most notable event was the arrival of a member of the groundstaff with bucket, spade and besom to deal with some wasps which had congregated at the Vauxhall End.

ESSEX v NORTHAMPTONSHIRE
At Chelmsford, June 13, 14, 15, 17, 1996

On the second day, spectators were briefly diverted when a muntjac fawn appeared from under the parked covers, jumped into the members' enclosure and then into the river. It was found later, safe but scared, in a nearby churchyard.

CRICKET IN CYPRUS
[1996]

There are three midweek leagues, involving 20 teams. Two or three native Cypriots play for Mouflons, a Limassol-based team, named after a wild sheep found in the Troodos Mountains.

CRICKET IN FRANCE
[1997]

Robin Marlar's ground (complete with turf wicket) at Mollans-sur-Ouveze, Provence, was wrecked by wild boar, who dug their snouts into the turf and almost ploughed it up. 'Hampshire Hogs on tour, I expect,' said Marlar. The ground has had to be temporarily abandoned.

ENGLAND v AUSTRALIA
Leeds, July 24, 25, 26, 27, 1997

Two men dressed in a pantomime-cow costume cavorted round the boundary, and were crash-tackled by officials after play: the man playing the rear end, Branco Risek, needed treatment in hospital. Brian Cheesman, a university lecturer dressed as a carrot, was frogmarched from the ground for 'drunken and abusive behaviour'. He vehemently denied the allegations. Mr Cheesman has been attending Headingley Tests in fancy dress since 1982.

SRI LANKA A v ENGLAND A
Kurunegala, January 30, February 1, 2, 3, 1998

Jayawardene batted for nearly five hours, and shared the limelight on the third day with a snake, said to be five feet long, which was hit by a ball struck to long-on. Sri Lanka A eventually declared 17 behind, and the players thereafter went through the motions.

TAMIL NADU v PUNJAB
Chennai, March 30, 31, April 1, 2, 3, 2000

Play was delayed for several minutes on the opening morning by a snake in the outfield, and for 20 minutes on the final morning by a swarm of bees, which stung spectators and caused the players to throw themselves to the ground, until the umpires decided to take an early lunch.

UTTAR PRADESH v VIDARBHA
Nagpur, December 28, 29, 30, 31, 2000

On the third day, play was delayed for 20 minutes by a mad dog on the field.

NATIONAL VILLAGE CHAMPIONSHIP
[2001]

Many clubs had difficulty staging games because of the foot-and-mouth epidemic. In North Yorkshire, Ingleby Greenhow settled their fixture with Middleton Tyas at darts.

DURHAM v NOTTINGHAMSHIRE
Chester-le-Street, May 30, 31, June 1, 2, 2001

On the rain-interrupted first day, Blewett had been distracted first by the bails coming off in the wind and fatally by three ducks waddling behind the umpire as Brinkley ran in.

SURREY v YORKSHIRE
Guildford, July 24, 25, 26, 27, 2002

Yorkshire were unable to muster enough second-innings runs to set a challenging target. They might have put more pressure on Surrey had it not been for a bizarre interlude when Blakey swept a four into the press tent. After the ball was fetched, Hollioake noticed some tooth marks; the culprit, it transpired, was Bumper, a Labrador who belonged to Geoffrey Dean from *The Times*. The damage prompted Hollioake to take the new ball – 21 overs after it had become available – and Surrey's seamers quickly despatched the Yorkshire tail.

CRICKET IN FINLAND
[2002]

The elements continue to make cricket in Finland a singular experience: a while back, play was stopped when an elk galloped out of the woods, and early in the 2002 season bowlers ran over snow on their run-ups.

CRICKET IN NAMIBIA
[2003]

Namibia hosted Zimbabwe A in September, winning the three-match one-day series but losing the two three-day games. At one stage,

Namibian and Zimbabwean players and umpires lay face down as a swarm of bees descended.

SUSSEX v YORKSHIRE
Arundel, June 27, 2004

Yorkshire won with 18.1 overs spare. They did so in dark blue kit, after Wood went out to toss in their intended yellow away shirt and was attacked by a swarm of insects.

Cricketers Behaving Badly

MIDDLESEX v THE AUSTRALIANS
Lord's, June 20, 21, 22, 1878

Midwinter was to have played for the Australians, and just before noon on the first day he was duly flannelled and practising at Lord's ready for play, but shortly after W. G. Grace arrived in hot haste from Kennington, claiming and obtaining Midwinter to play for Gloucestershire v Surrey, which match was commenced that day on The Oval. It was rumoured W. G. Grace acted on a prior made agreement; be that as it may Midwinter played that day for Gloucestershire, and never again played for the Australians on the tour.

NOTES BY THE EDITOR, 1942
VARYING STRENGTH

The rise and decline of great players affected the strength of the sides to such an extent that Gloucestershire have not once finished first since 1877. That was the season when Midwinter, who was born at Cirencester and had come back from Australia, appeared as the first professional in the Gloucestershire ranks. He returned to Australia in the winter, played in the two matches against J. Lillywhite's England team and started the next summer with the Australians captained by David Gregory. He took part in five matches, but he was induced to resume playing for Gloucestershire 'in dramatic fashion', as Sydney Pardon used to describe. The Australians were at Lord's for the match with Middlesex; Gloucestershire, on arriving at The Oval for their game with Surrey, decided that they must have Midwinter. In order to impress a man nearly 6 feet 3 inches in height and weighing about 15 stones, W. G. Grace, the Gloucestershire captain, himself a heavyweight, and E. M. Grace, the Coroner, took with them J. A. Bush, comparable to Midwinter as a giant. In a four-wheeled cab they drove to Lord's and brought back Midwinter. Weighty argument had the desired effect! Midwinter went to and from Australia for several consecutive seasons. He considered himself an Australian and once said: 'I made a mistake in deserting the first Australian eleven of 1878.' He played for Alfred Shaw's team in the four matches against Australia in 1881 and 1882, and appeared for W. L. Murdoch's 1884 team against England at Manchester, Lord's and The Oval, so representing both these countries in matches against each other – a unique distinction.

W. G. GRACE

A. G. Steel writes: W. G. has, so it goes without saying, a thorough knowledge of the game, and I recollect well in the summer of 1878 an incident which well illustrates the fact. North v South was being played at Lord's. Barlow, the Lancashire professional, was batting, and W. G. was fielding point. Now Barlow had a trick of tapping the ball away after he had played it, and occasionally, in order to excite a laugh from the onlookers, would scamper down the pitch for a yard or two and then back again. On this occasion he just stopped the ball and it lay by his crease; he then tapped it towards point, and perhaps thinking he would hustle that fielder, he went through his performance of dashing down the pitch and back again. He must have been thoroughly upset by the action of point, who, ignoring the ball, quietly asked the umpire, 'How's that for hitting the ball twice?' and out Barlow had to go – a lesson which he never forgot.

E. J. ('TIGER') SMITH
(1886–1979)

For a time he was seconded to the MCC. It was during this period that he met W. G. Grace, and played in several matches for and against Grace's London County Eleven. 'Do you know what he'd do if he thought you weren't any good?' chuckled 'Tiger'. 'He'd go out and buy a rabbit and put it in your cricketing bag.'

THE AUSTRALIANS v NOTTINGHAMSHIRE
Nottingham, June 8, 9, 10, 1882

The only serious unpleasantness during the tour occurred during the progress of this match, and it must be admitted the Colonists had just cause for irritation. It appears that on arriving at Nottingham from Bradford, at about one o'clock in the morning, the Australians were unable to obtain the rooms which had been engaged for them, and in consequence did not get to bed until nearly three. This circumstance, as annoying as it was to tired travellers, would probably soon have been forgotten, but when the interval for luncheon arrived the Colonists found that no places had been reserved for them at the table, a piece of unaccountable carelessness on the part of the executive, which, coming after the mishap overnight, led to an unfriendly interchange of words between the Secretary of the County Club and Murdoch and other members of the team, and to a correspondence in the papers, which made the matter more regrettable.

DERBYSHIRE v SURREY
Derby, July 17, 18, 1894

Before the commencement of the match some unpleasantness occurred, and Hulme, though present, refused to go into the field, having some personal grievance against one of the players. He did not take part in the game, but the little dispute was made up later on, and he appeared in the concluding engagements of the county.

MEETING OF COUNTY SECRETARIES
December 11, 1894

MR. MURDOCH (Sussex) had a strong opinion – he spoke from experience and suggested the matter for the consideration of the counties – that it was desirable to provide a room for umpires. At present they went into the players' room and were subjected to all sorts of remarks and sometimes abuse; and no matter how honest an umpire might be – and he believed they were all honest – they could hardly fail to be affected. If umpires were kept apart from the cricketers a great deal of good would be done.

MIDDLESEX IN 1907

One incident during the season gave rise to a great deal of discussion and not a little ill-feeling. We refer, of course, to the abandonment on the 23rd of July 1907 of the match with Lancashire. The details of this most unfortunate affair will be fresh in the memory of everyone who follows cricket at all closely. A lot of rain fell on the first day and in such time as was available Lancashire scored 57 for one wicket. At the ordinary time for resuming the following morning play was quite out of the question, and as events turned out it would have been much better if the umpires, who from time to time inspected the pitch, had early in the day declared cricket impracticable. As it was the people who had paid for admission became very impatient at the long delay, and after stumps had at last been pulled up some of them went so far as to trample on the wicket. A lengthy consultation and discussion by the captains followed, and after six o'clock MacLaren handed the following official statement to the Press:

> Owing to the pitch having been deliberately torn up by the public, I, as captain of the Lancashire eleven, cannot see my way to continue the game, the groundsman bearing me out that the wicket could not again be put right.
>
> A. C. MacLaren

Opinion was very much divided as to the action MacLaren took, a letter of indignant protest being addressed to the *Field* by Mr R. D. Walker, the Middlesex president. The actual damage to the pitch did not, it was stated, amount to more than one rather deep heel mark.

REFLECTIONS BY PATSY HENDREN
[1937]

You know what they say about cards: bad beginning, good ending. Well, my first county match was one in which I did not get an innings! That was in 1907 against Lancashire at Lord's, the game being abandoned before lunch on the second day. There were naturally unusual circumstances. After heavy rain, a drizzle set in, but the crowd – allowed, as they were then, on the playing-area – gathered in front of the Pavilion and clamoured for cricket. In the middle of all the rumpus, somebody got on to the pitch itself and, accidentally or not, stuck the ferrule of an umbrella into the turf. When this was discovered by Mr. Archie MacLaren, the Lancashire captain, he refused to play, even if a fresh wicket were cut out. So there was nothing for it but to pack up and go home.

ENGLAND v AUSTRALIA
Trent Bridge, June 10, 11, 13, 14, 1938

When Australia followed on 247 behind, batting of a much different character was seen. Brown and Fingleton adopted 'stone-walling' tactics which called forth mild 'barracking' from some of the spectators and Fingleton followed the extraordinary procedure of stepping away from his wicket, taking off his gloves and laying down his bat.

MIDDLESEX v DERBYSHIRE
Lord's, August 24, 25, 26, 1949

The equanimity of the Lord's Pavilion was disturbed when Gladwin, after being run-out by his partner, accidentally put his bat through the dressing-room window.

NOTTINGHAM v GLAMORGAN
Nottingham, June 30, July 2, 3, 1957

So slowly did Glamorgan score on the first day that Simpson, the Nottinghamshire captain, bowled an over of lobs as a protest and, following this incident, Glamorgan lost four wickets for 11 runs.

INDIA v ENGLAND
Madras, January 10, 11, 13, 14, 15, 1962

Brown would have played instead of David Smith but for a cut middle finger on the right hand. India did not agree to his playing with sticking plaster on it.

NOTES BY THE EDITOR, 1974
THE FAGG INCIDENT

While on the subject of captaincy, it was regrettable that Kanhai showed such open dissent on the field at Edgbaston when umpire Fagg turned down an appeal against Boycott for a catch at the wicket. Fagg threatened to quit the match and indeed it took a lot of persuasion behind the scenes before he agreed to resume next morning after missing the first over. The reaction of Fagg while at boiling point met with much criticism, and it would certainly have been better had he grappled with the situation through the Test and County Cricket Board representative who was on hand for just such an occurrence rather than in the Press, but at least it brought the matter to a head. For too long, and not only in this country, players from junior to senior standing have been reflecting their dislike at umpires' decisions almost with disdain. Now the TCCB have taken a firm stand by declaring at their December meeting that umpires will receive full support in reporting, as is their duty, any pressurising on the field. I am afraid Kanhai lost his way, of all places, on the ground where for years he has proved such a popular figure. Maybe he did so in his anxiety not to let slip any chance of capitalizing on his team's victory in the first of the three Tests, but that cannot excuse his behaviour. Captains more than hold the key to clearing up a bad habit which has no place in the game of cricket.

NEW ZEALAND v ENGLAND
Christchurch, February 24, 25, 26, 28, March 1, 1978

England had two and a half hours batting on the fourth evening during which New Zealand bowled 22 overs and there was an unfortunate incident when Chatfield without warning, ran out Randall, the non-striker. Chatfield ran in normally, stopped, and took off the bails under-arm to the acute embarrassment of the majority of the spectators. The view in an angry English camp was that, if Chatfield had continued with his normal overarm action, Randall would still have been in his ground. In the English first innings there had been some gallery-playing action by Hadlee against two batsmen. He held the ball after completing his action, and it hardly needs adding that the game would be in a constant state of disruption if bowlers made a habit of such tactics.

PAKISTAN v INDIA
Faisalabad, October 16, 17, 18, 20, 21, 1978

Although the match was played for the most part in good humour, there was an unsavoury incident late on the fourth day at the start of Pakistan's second innings. During discussions that followed the warning by umpire Shakoor Rana of Mohinder Amarnath for following through into the proscribed area of the pitch, Gavaskar, the Indian vice-captain, used insulting language against the umpire concerned. Mr Rana and his colleague refused to go out the next morning until action was taken, and play was delayed by eleven minutes while a compromise was reached.

PAKISTAN IN AUSTRALIA, 1978–79

Brian Osborne writes: Derogatory comments by Asif Iqbal on the eve of the Melbourne Test on the standards of the Australian and England teams in their series created ill-feeling that manifested itself in several incidents during the two Tests. These can only be described as unsportsmanlike and completely opposed to the best traditions of the game, even if they technically complied with the Laws of Cricket. In Melbourne, Hogg was run out by Miandad, who moved from silly point to break the wicket after the batsman, having played a defensive stroke a short distance down the wicket, left his crease to inspect the wicket. Although Hogg was recalled by Mushtaq, umpire Harvey confirmed his earlier decision. Hogg promptly struck down the stumps before leaving the wicket. At Perth, fast bowler Hurst ran out Sikander when he was 'backing up' ahead of the delivery – thus breaking a troublesome last wicket partnership with Asif who, in turn, wrecked his own wicket in the same style as Hogg. Then in the final Australian innings, the acting captain, Hilditch, at the non-striker's end, picked up the ball after a return from a fieldsman, handed it in a helpful manner to bowler Sarfraz, and was immediately the victim of an appeal and dismissal for 'handled the ball'. All three incidents were much to be deprecated.

WORCESTERSHIRE v SOMERSET
Worcester, May 23, 24, 1979

Worcestershire beat Somerset by ten wickets when the Somerset captain, Rose, sacrificed all known cricketing principles by deliberately losing the game. His declaration after one over from Holder, who bowled a no-ball to concede the only run, enabled Somerset to maintain their superior striking rate in the group.

In the end, Worcestershire and Somerset went forward when Glamorgan's final match was rained off, thus preventing the Welsh county from joining the other two teams with nine points. Rose won the battle of mathematics but lost all the goodwill which Somerset had gained by playing attractive cricket in the preceding years. Worcestershire, embarrassed if not totally angered, refunded admission money to 100 paying spectators after Turner had scored two singles to complete their victory in a match which lasted for sixteen deliveries and only twenty minutes, including the ten minutes between the innings. Worcestershire chairman, Mr Geoffrey Lampard commented: 'It is a great pity when the supreme game of cricket is brought down to this level'. The TCCB met at Lord's on June 1 and Somerset, for bringing the game into disrepute, were disqualified from the Benson and Hedges Cup by seventeen votes to one (Derbyshire).

PAKISTAN v WEST INDIES
Multan, December 30, 31, 1980, January 2, 3, 4, 1981

The start of the fourth and final Test, played on a new Test ground, was delayed by the late arrival of an umpire. The match was marred on the second day by Clarke's disgraceful action in throwing a brick into the crowd. The spectators erupted and play was held up for twenty-five minutes until Kallicharran appealed to the crowd on bended knee to restore order.

AUSTRALIA v INDIA
Melbourne, February 7, 8, 9, 10, 11, 1981

This was a sensational match, not only for Australia's astonishing collapse in the second innings against an Indian attack that was badly handicapped by injuries. India had come near to forfeiting the match on the previous day when their captain, Gavaskar, so sharply disagreed with an lbw decision against himself that he wanted to call off the contest. The incident took place in India's second innings, at the end of an opening partnership of 165 between Gavaskar and Chauhan. When Gavaskar was given out by umpire Whitehead, he first indicated that he had edged the ball on to his pad, and then, as he walked past Chauhan he urged him to leave the field with him. Fortunately the manager of the Indian team, Wing Commander S. K. Durrani, intervened, meeting the in-coming pair at the gate and ordering Chauhan to continue his innings.

THE PAKISTANIS IN AUSTRALIA, 1981–82

The confrontation between Miandad and Lillee was one of the most undignified incidents in Test history. Miandad, batting to Lillee, had turned a ball to the on side and was in the course of completing a comfortable single when he was obstructed by Lillee. In the ensuing fracas Lillee kicked Miandad, who responded by shaping to strike him with his bat. The Australian team imposed a $200 fine (£120 approx.) on Lillee and sought an apology from Miandad for his part in the affair.

However, the umpires, who had assisted in quelling the incident, objected to the penalty as being too lenient and the matter was dealt with at a Melbourne hearing before Mr R. Merriman, the coordinator of the Australian Cricket Board's cricket sub-committee. His ruling was that Lillee's penalty, set by the players, was not sufficient and he imposed a suspension from Australia's two ensuing one-day internationals – against Pakistan and West Indies. No apology was forthcoming from Miandad, whose participation in the incident was also referred to in the umpires' report.

POT-HOLES

Customs men confiscated a consignment of cricket bats which arrived at Heathrow Airport from India in August 1982 and were found to have been hollowed out and filled with cannabis. Charges were subsequently brought.

SOUTH AUSTRALIA v WESTERN AUSTRALIA
Adelaide, December 2, 3, 4, 5, 1983

Set 218 to win, Western Australia were soon under threat from the weather, and it was because of rain that the match finished controversially. After the umpires had brought the players off in light drizzle, they were advised by Col Egar, a former Test umpire and now a South Australian luminary, to get play started again. This angered Hookes, the South Australian captain, as much as it pleased Hughes, leading Western Australia, who were thus enabled to win, the final runs coming in quite heavy rain. With Hughes exacerbating a tense situation by sitting on the boundary's edge and making provocative remarks, and Hookes showing the umpires a copy of the Laws, neither captain emerged from the incident with credit.

INDIA v ENGLAND
Calcutta, December 31, 1984, January 1, 3, 4, 5, 1985

Smog and rain, which restricted play to twenty minutes on the second day, followed by Gavaskar's perverse decision to continue India's innings from 417 for seven at lunch time on the fourth, made certain of a pointless and tedious draw. Gavaskar's lack of ambition, or evident direction, while Azharuddin and Shastri were adding 214 for the fifth wicket at under 2 runs an over, so incensed the crowd that there were fears a riot might develop. That section of the crowd nearest the pavilion hooted and booed, shouting 'Gavaskar down, Gavaskar out' when the Indian captain made a brief appearance outside the dressing-room while Prabhakar and Chetan Sharma were batting at a snail's pace, and he was pelted with fruit when eventually he led India out to field, the game being held up for eight minutes while groundstaff cleared the outfield. Gower helped prompt his declaration – even then reluctant – twenty minutes after lunch with three overs of derisive off-breaks, while Edmonds took a leaf out of Warwick Armstrong's book at The Oval in 1921 by reading a newspaper as the captain waited at his mark to bowl. Gavaskar subsequently denied that police had warned him there was a threat to law and order should he delay the declaration any longer, though it was broadcast as a fact by an Indian commentator on BBC radio.

SRI LANKA v PAKISTAN
Colombo, February 23, 24, 25, 26, 27, 1986

The match was over soon after lunch, even though some 30 minutes had been lost when the umpires, followed by the Sri Lankan batsmen, Dias and Ranatunga, returned to the pavilion in protest at the abuse delivered by the fieldsmen when an appeal for a catch, from Ranatunga to forward short leg, was turned down. Play resumed after Imran apologised to the umpires.

SRI LANKA v PAKISTAN
Colombo, March 14, 15, 16, 18, 1986

Two controversial incidents, in addition to disputed decisions, marred the third day. The replacement of a damaged ball after sixteen overs of Pakistan's second innings produced an objection from the batsmen when an umpire began rubbing the new ball on the ground to effect 'a similar amount of wear'. They reported the matter to the Pakistan manager, who came on to the field of play with a 1985 *Wisden* to show the relevant Law to the umpires. Later Miandad, angered by the lbw decision which dismissed him and riled by the jeering of the crowd, mounted the stairs of the pavilion in search of a spectator who had thrown a stone at him.

INDIA v WEST INDIES
Nagpur, December 8, 1987

A match of fluctuating fortunes was marred by a controversial umpiring decision which brought about the dismissal of Vengsarkar. Umpire Mehra first turned down an appeal for a slip catch by Richards, whereupon the West Indies captain appealed to the square-leg umpire. When he indicated that he was unsighted and could not give a ruling, Richard's tantrum virtually coerced Mehra into reversing his decision.

AUSTRALIA v NEW ZEALAND
Melbourne, December 26, 27, 28, 29, 30, 1987

Put in to bat, the New Zealanders had reached 119 for one when, half an hour before tea, Jones edged a delivery from McDermott and watched as the Australian wicket-keeper, Dyer, rolled over then showed the ball in his raised right hand, indicating a clean catch. Umpire Crafter, sensing something was amiss, delayed his decision until umpire French at square leg indicated that the ball had carried. But television replays showed the ball bouncing out of Dyer's gloves and on to the ground, with the wicket-keeper scooping the ball back into his gloves before appealing.

CRICKET IN INDIA, 1987–88

This review cannot pass without mention of the ban imposed on Dilip Vengsarkar who, having been elevated to the captaincy of the Indian team for the series against West Indies, broke his contract with the Indian Board by writing comments on the matches for newspapers. He was suspended from first-class cricket for six months and so missed the Ranji Trophy knockout matches. He was also omitted from the Indian team for the Sharjah Cup tournament in March, as were Manoj Prabhakar and Maninder Singh following their unseemly clash during the Steel Trophy tournament in Delhi. Maninder, playing for the Steel Authority Club, and Prabhakar, of the Banking Sports Club, came to blows after an exchange of words on the field of play. The Delhi and District Association, to whom both owed allegiance, severely reprimanded them, and the Indian selectors supported the association's action.

CRICKET IN INDIA, 1990–91

The violent action, senseless yet far from unprovoked, of Rashid Patel of West Zone, who went after Raman Lamba of North Zone, stump in hand, will be remembered as the most shameful moment in the history of Indian cricket. It occurred on the final afternoon of the five-day match in Jamshedpur, after Patel had come down the pitch to aim a head-high full toss at the batsman, Lamba. Nor was it the only controversy of a game in which senior players questioned the umpires' decisions and berated officials. Yet in the end, the Board of Control for Cricket in India seemed to draw a veil over the acrimony which found its final expression in the beamer attack, for none of the players was disciplined except for Patel and Lamba, who were banned for thirteen and ten months respectively. The sequel to the violence on the pitch was a riot in the crowd, which resulted in the covers and anything else suitable being set alight, bringing the match to a premature conclusion.

NEW ZEALAND v PAKISTAN
Napier, December 28, 1992

The match was overshadowed by an incident which led to Aqib Javed becoming the first player to be suspended for breaches of the ICC Code of Conduct. New Zealand were chasing 137 and had lost both openers for 30 when Jones gave a lobbed, gloved slip catch off a short-pitched delivery from Aqib. Umpire Aldridge called a no-ball, judging that it was above shoulder-height, a verdict supported by television replays. After the match, Aldridge reported the bowler to the referee, Peter Burge. The non-striker, Crowe, and a nearby fieldsman, Ramiz Raja, attended a 75-minute hearing, where Crowe said Aqib had called the umpire an 'effing cheat'. To Aqib's defence that he was talking to himself, he commented: 'It was a funny thing to call yourself.' Burge suspended the bowler for the next international.

WARWICKSHIRE v MIDDLESEX
Birmingham, July 15, 16, 17, 19, 1993

Tufnell's match was not entirely happy. He was incensed when Moles scored four from a free hit at a ball which had slipped from his hand and run to square leg; it became six through the two-run penalty for a no-ball. Later that over, when Ratcliffe declined to walk before he was formally given out for a catch at the wicket, Tufnell lost his temper, shouted abuse at Ratcliffe and had to be restrained by team-mates.

BOMBAY v MAHARASHTRA
Solapur, December 23, 24, 25, 26, 1994

S. V. Manjrekar was sent off the field by umpire V. N. Kulkarni for abusive language.

LEAGUE CRICKET IN ENGLAND AND WALES, 1995

The Essex League threw up one of the season's more bizarre controversies, when John Lever of Ilford – *the* John Lever – was given out handled the ball when he picked it up after a defensive shot and threw it back to the bowler. Gary Neicho, the South Woodford captain, appealed from mid-off and Lever was given out. He was disgusted and Neicho was criticised in both the local and national press; he insisted the ball was still rolling towards the stumps when Lever picked it up.

KARACHI BLUES v LAHORE CITY
Karachi, November 20, 21, 22, 1995

Karachi Blues won by default after Lahore City conceded the match.

Lahore City captain Aamer Malik called back his batsmen, alleging that Karachi Blues had secretly replaced the ball during the drinks interval. The umpires and referee rejected the accusation, but Lahore City refused to continue.

INDIA v PAKISTAN
Toronto, September 14, 1997

India's emphatic victory was overshadowed by the fracas in which Inzamam-ul-Haq accosted a spectator who had been taunting him using a megaphone. Play was held up for 35 minutes and referee Jackie Hendriks suspended Inzamam for two matches. Assault charges against Inzamam and the spectator, Shiva Kumar Thind, were subsequently dropped.

SOMERSET v ESSEX
Bath, June 17, 18, 19, 20, 1998

As the rain fell on the second day, Somerset dressing-room high spirits spilled out on to the field: Mushtaq Ahmed was manhandled on to the pitch and tied to a chair; it was said to be revenge for his own practical jokes.

ZIMBABWE v SRI LANKA
Harare, November 26-30, 1999

On the fourth day, Goodwin and Andy Flower showed tremendous fighting spirit and, as they survived well into the afternoon session, the Sri Lankans grew increasingly frustrated. So hysterical did their appeals become that the match referee, Jackie Hendriks, spoke to them during the tea interval, after which their behaviour was impeccable.

By then, however, Zimbabwe's defences had been breached in a way that caused great offence. Goodwin and Flower had not long reached their century partnership when Goodwin played the last delivery of Vaas's over, the fifth before tea, back to the bowler. Vaas, rather than pick the ball up, kicked it back towards the slips, Goodwin himself aiming a light-hearted kick as it passed him before he wandered down the pitch to do some 'gardening'. But the umpire had not called 'over', and Dilshan, picking up the ball, threw down his wicket.

MIDDLESEX v ESSEX
Southgate, July 18, 19, 20, 21, 2002

A bad-tempered game finally petered out into one of the most boring draws imaginable. The second-division leaders, Middlesex, were so determined not to let third-placed Essex gain any ground that they batted until tea on the final day, setting a meaningless target of 524. Essex had already registered disgust by sitting down in the outfield to eat ice creams during a pointedly unhurried afternoon drinks break. Before the tedium had come rancour. On the first day, Cowan was warned for intimidatory bowling, and on the second both teams became embroiled as Tufnell and Irani traded abuse. The umpires had to intervene, and the sides were reported for bad behaviour.

WINDWARD ISLANDS v GUYANA
Roseau, January 23, 24, 25, 26, 2004

Guyana lost all ten wickets for 50 runs on the final day to go down to their third successive defeat. Afterwards, it was reported that a fight broke out on their team bus, and the Windwards scorer, who was also the mayor of Roseau, had to threaten two players with arrest.

MIDDLESEX v SURREY
Lord's, April 21, 22, 23, 24, 2004

Koenig, out for 62, was so annoyed he hurled his helmet at a dressing-room chair, only for it to bounce and shatter a window. The seats below were showered with broken glass, but fortunately their occupants had decided to go for lunch early.

GLAMORGAN v DERBYSHIRE
Cardiff, May 3, 4, 5, 6, 2006

On the opening day, Derbyshire's behaviour made them look far from winners. Taylor, who had just celebrated a maiden Championship century, was run out after taking a single only to find his partner, Hassan Adnan, had not budged. He then threatened Adnan with his bat.

Doing the Right Thing

SUSSEX v LANCASHIRE
Brighton, August 16, 17, 18, 1897

Before being taken ill, Bland sent down three overs for 13 runs and consequently got his name on the score sheet, but Mr MacLaren, the Lancashire Captain, allowed another man to play in his place. It was, of course, a sportsmanlike action, but set up a very dangerous precedent, and was generally disapproved of at the time.

ENGLAND v THE DOMINIONS
Lord's, August 2, 3, 1943

After tea Constantine played in his own aggressive style, but from a hard drive Leslie Compton caught him with the left hand at full stretch while leaning on the pavilion rails with feet on the ground. This perfectly fair catch caused much criticism as the ball might have been over the boundary, but Constantine knew the rules and said 'That is cricket'.

MIDDLESEX v SOMERSET
Lord's, May 10, 12, 13, 1947

Somerset won by one wicket. Despite a close-set field, defence still prevailed until Tremlett lifted an almost straight drive into the members' stand, and, with two 3s to the on, he finished the match. The Middlesex team lined up and cheered as their successful opponents went to the pavilion.

ESSEX v NOTTINGHAMSHIRE
Ilford, June 7, 8, 9, 1950

Sime, the Nottinghamshire captain, was involved in an unusual incident in his second innings. He was given out to what seemed a catch in the slips and returned to the pavilion, but Insole, the Essex captain, requested him to resume.

ENGLAND v NEW ZEALAND
Christchurch, March 17, 19, 20, 21, 1951

Early in the England innings occurred an incident believed to be unique in Test cricket. Washbrook, when 13 and the total 27, was given out leg-before, but after Hadlee, the New Zealand captain, held a short consultation with the umpire he was recalled when on his way to the pavilion. Apparently Hadlee, who had stopped Washbrook on his way out, told the umpire that he felt certain Washbrook had hit the ball on to his pad. The ethics of this action caused considerable discussion.

HUBERT PRESTON
[1868-1960]

Neville Cardus writes: I didn't dare go into the Lord's press box during my first season as a cricket writer. One afternoon, Hubert Preston saw me as I sat on the Green Bank scribbling my message. 'Why don't you come into the press box?' he said, in his own brisk, rapidly articulated way. He took me by the arm and led me up the steep iron steps. The tea interval wasn't over yet. Preston introduced me to Sydney Pardon, who then introduced me to the other members of the Press Box, some of them life members . . . Each made a courteous bow to me; it was like a levee. Pardon pointed to a seat in the back row. In time, he assured me, I would graduate to a front place among the elect. Hubert Preston was, with Pardon and Stewart Caine, the most courteous and best-mannered man ever to be seen in a press box. Stewart Caine would actually bow to me and give me precedence into a gentlemen's lavatory.

T. N. PEARCE'S XI v AUSTRALIANS
Scarborough, September 6, 7, 8, 1961

This match yielded 1,499 runs, the second largest aggregate for a three-day fixture. It was played in a light-hearted manner with no ducks because each batsman was given an easy ball to get off the mark and no lbw decisions because there was no appeal when the ball hit the pads.

ENGLAND v AUSTRALIA
Old Trafford, July 23, 24, 25, 27, 28, 1964

When 203, Simpson could have been run out backing-up if Titmus, about to bowl, had not been chivalrously inclined, and the Middlesex bowler inappropriately suffered when the Australian captain, bestirring himself again, hit 14 off him in one over.

SOUTH AFRICA v ENGLAND
Cape Town, January 1, 2, 4, 5, 6, 1965

Long after the unenterprising cricket of this Test is forgotten, people will talk of two incidents which brought to a head the question of whether batsmen should 'walk'. With close-in fieldsmen convinced both times that umpire Warner was wrong to turn down appeals for catches, the first at short leg, the second by the wicket-keeper, Barlow of South Africa stood his ground and Barrington of England made his way to the pavilion. Parfitt felt he had caught Barlow when that batsman was 41 runs towards his 138 of the first day and Barrington tickled the ball to Lindsay when 49 and looking set for a big score. So both happenings could be said to have had a big bearing on the way the game went.

The England players were so piqued at the Barlow incident that they did not applaud his century, an action which later produced an apology.

AUSTRALIA v ENGLAND
Melbourne, March 12, 13, 14, 16, 17 1977

When Randall was 161, umpire Brooks gave him out, caught at the wicket. Immediately Marsh intimated that he had not completed the catch before dropping the ball. After consultation, the umpire called Randall back. Would that this spirit was always so!

INDIA v ENGLAND
Bombay, February 15, 16, 17, 18, 19, 1980

Botham, batting for 206 minutes and hitting seventeen 4s, scored 114 in an innings which was responsible and yet not lacking in enterprise. His stand of 171 with Taylor was England's best-ever sixth-wicket partnership against India. Taylor remained entrenched until the third day was more than an hour old and altogether scored 43 in a stay of four and a half hours. Yet their stand could have been cut short at only 85 when umpire Hanumantha Rao upheld an appeal against Taylor for a catch behind the wicket, off Kapil Dev. Taylor hesitated and protested at the decision. Viswanath, the Indian captain, who was fielding at first slip, was as certain as the batsman that there had been no contact and persuaded the umpire to rescind his verdict.

CRICKET'S ROLE, 1984

'Cricket? It civilises people and creates good gentlemen. I want everyone to play cricket in Zimbabwe. I want ours to be a nation of gentlemen.

President Robert Mugabe

MIDDLESEX v NOTTINGHAMSHIRE
Lord's, July 10, 11, 12 1985

Randall 'walked' when the umpire had not given him out in Nottinghamshire's first innings, which Williams ended with three wickets in a span of ten balls.

NEW ZEALAND v AUSTRALIA
Auckland, March 13, 14, 15, 16, 17, 1986

At 62 Rutherford was given out, but Zoehrer signalled that the catch had not been properly made, Border chivalrously waved him back, and New Zealand finished the day 85 for one.

GETTY'S GIFTS TO CRICKET

J. Paul Getty II, who in 1985 contributed £1.5 million towards the cost of the new Mound Stand at Lord's, made further generous donations to cricket in 1986. These included £380,000 to help create the Arundel Castle Cricket Foundation, the aim of which is to provide cricket and cricket coaching for young people who might otherwise have little or no opportunity to play the game. The Foundation is to be administered by J. R. T. Barclay, until last season the captain of Sussex. Other donations by Getty included £10,000 each to Kent, as a contribution towards the cost of the new stand at Canterbury, to Gloucestershire, for help with the cost of a new cricket school at the Phoenix County Ground in Bristol, and to Leicestershire, in support of an indoor sports centre.

AUSTRALIA v NEW ZEALAND

Melbourne, December 26, 27, 28, 29, 30, 1987

The last Australian pair, McDermott and Whitney, held out for 4.5 overs to claim a draw and give Australia the Trans-Tasman Trophy for the first time. When Whitney, playing in his first Test since 1981, dug out Hadlee's final ball of the match, the New Zealand fast bowler walked down the pitch to the exuberant batsman, put an arm around his shoulder and shook his hand.

YORKSHIRE v WARWICKSHIRE

Sheffield, June 20, 21, 22, 1990

The match was contested in a very good spirit, both Moles and Moxon walking without hesitation for the thinnest of edges.

ENGLAND v AUSTRALIA

Lord's, June 19, 20, 21, 22, 23, 1997

Thorpe almost went before he had scored, but wicket-keeper Healy was uncertain about his 'catch' and told the umpires so, prompting a burst of applause from umpire Shepherd.

LANCASHIRE v SUSSEX
Lord's, August 26, 2006

Kirtley thudded one into the pads, and Loye did something rather strange: after an lbw shout, he walked.

JONTY RHODES (b 1969)

Enjoyment is paramount. 'It is a game,' he says. 'I play cricket because I love it.' Religion, though, is crucial in his life. He says he will always walk if he knows he is out, and recall a batsman if he takes a catch on the bounce. 'The Lord doesn't like cheating,' he says. Such a policy makes bad decisions doubly cruel, but Rhodes says: 'Averages are not everything, it's also about that old thing of how you played the game.'

Extreme Bowling

ALL THE 20 WICKETS, 1872

Mr C. Absolon – an old and liberal supporter of Metropolitan cricket and cricketers – was the grey-haired hero of this very successful bowling feat, i.e.: – having a hand in the downfall of all the twenty wickets; he bowled ten, two hit wicket, six were caught from his bowling, and he caught out the remaining two. The match made famous by this bowling of Mr Absolon's was Wood Green v United Willesden, played at Wood Green, July 21, 1872. Wood Green won by an innings and 45 runs.

MR FREDERICK AITKEN LEESTON-SMITH
(1854–1903)

He was a powerful hitter, a middle-paced round-armed bowler, and generally fielded at point. In a match between Weston-super-Mare and Thornbury, he once hit E. M. Grace for four 6s from consecutive balls, a performance which the latter has described as follows: – 'F. L. Cole made 1 off my first ball, F. A. Leeston-Smith 6 off the second, 6 off third, 6 off fourth, 6 off fifth, when the umpire said, 'I am afraid it is over, Doctor.' I said, 'Shut up, I am going to have another,' and off this one he was stumped. Weston-super-Mare had to follow their innings. Leeston-Smith came in first, and the first ball I bowled him he hit for 6. The second also went for 6, but off the third he was stumped again.

SIR STANLEY JACKSON
(1880–1947)

Wilfred Rhodes, now 70 years of age, wrote: As a bowler he used spin and variation of pace with a clever slow one. On one occasion, when bowling to G. L. Jessop at Cambridge, he sent up his slower ball, which was hit out of the field over the trees. Schofield Haigh, fielding

mid-on, was laughing, and Stanley, turning round, said to him, 'What are you laughing at?' Haigh replied, 'Your slow ball, sir.' Stanley: 'It was a good one, wasn't it?'

FROM DOCTOR GRACE TO PETER MAY
[1958]

Herbert Strudwick writes: On the occasion of my first Gentlemen and Players match, I asked Albert Trott how I could find his fast ball, which he disguised so well. 'You'll soon find it,' Albert told me. It was some time before he bowled it and when he did it just missed the leg-stump and hit me full toss on the left foot. I was hopping round in great pain when Albert came up to me. 'You found it all right then,' he said.

BIRTH OF THE GOOGLY

B. J. T. Bosanquet writes: Somewhere about the year 1897 I was playing a game with a tennis ball, known as 'Twisti-Twosti.' The object was to bounce the ball on a table so that your opponent sitting opposite could not catch it. It soon occurred to me that if one could pitch a ball which broke in a certain direction and with more or less the same delivery make the next ball go in the opposite direction, one would mystify one's opponent. After a little experimenting I managed to do this, and it was so successful that I practised the same thing with a soft ball at 'Stump-cricket.' From this I progressed to a cricket ball, and about 1899 I had become a 'star turn' for the luncheon interval during our matches at Oxford. That is, the most famous batsman on the opposing side was enticed into a net and I was brought up to bowl him two or three leg-breaks. These were followed by an 'off-break' with more or less the same action. If this pitched on the right place it probably hit him on the knee, everyone shrieked with laughter, and I was led away and locked up for the day.

During this and the following year I devoted a great deal of time to practising the googly at the nets, and occasionally bowled in unimportant matches. The first public recognition we obtained was in July, 1900, for Middlesex v Leicestershire at Lord's. An unfortunate individual (I believe it was Coe) had made 98 when he was clean bowled by a fine specimen which bounced four times. The incident was rightly treated as a joke, and was the subject of ribald comment, but this small beginning marked the start of what came to be termed a revolution in bowling.

JOHN WILLIAM HITCH
(1886–1965)

The Surrey and England right-arm fast bowler. He had an unusual hesitant run-up in which his approach to the crease was punctuated by two or three hops. More than once he broke a stump, and at the Oval in 1921 he sent a bail 55 yards one foot in bowling A. R. Tanner of Middlesex.

ENGLAND v SOUTH AFRICA
Birmingham, June 14, 16, 17, 1924

The sensation of the match came on the second day. Gilligan's figures of six wickets for 7 runs have never been equalled. He bowled very fast and with any amount of fire. Three times during the innings, he took a wicket immediately after sending down a no-ball.

NOTES BY THE EDITOR, 1926

Just as the Almanack is going to press comes a letter from Hobart, stating that in a match there between New Town and North-West Hobart 'A' Grade on November 21, 1925, A.O. Burrows of New Town bowled one of his opponents with a ball which sent the bail 83 yards 1 foot 9 inches. The statement is vouched for by no fewer than half a dozen different men associated with the club or the other, among those being Joe Darling, the famous left handed batsman who captained Australia in this country in 1899, 1902 and 1905, and who is now president of the New Town Club. Previously the record was

70½ yards by A. F. Morcom for Bedfordshire against Suffolk at Luton in 1908.

WORCESTERSHIRE v AUSTRALIANS
Worcester, April 30, May 2, 3, 1938

McCormick, the fast bowler, repeatedly went over the crease and during his first three overs was no-balled nineteen times by umpire Baldwin. His first over actually comprised fourteen balls and the second over fifteen. Trying to hook one of the no-balls, Bull turned it against his face and received a terrific blow over the right eye, causing him to retire.

MISCELLANEA
[1944]

W. H. Chinnery, who, for Orsett (Essex) on May 15 and 22, 1943, took all ten wickets in successive matches, for 36 runs against Jurgens at Purfleet and for 42 runs against Hornchurch at Orsett, was presented with the balls with which he accomplished these performances, believed to constitute a record, at the annual meeting of the club last April.

MCC v QUEENSLAND
Brisbane, November 24, 25, 27, 28, 1950

MCC were shown a score-book containing a remarkable feat by the opposing opening batsman, Mackay. Playing for Virginia School against Sherwood School in the Semi-Final of the Queensland C.A. Shield on November 10, 1939, Mackay took all ten wickets for 53 and scored 367 not out.

AUSTRALIAN BOWLER'S FEAT
[1960]

Geoffrey Jinkins of the North Melbourne club achieved an astounding bowling feat in a Grade One match. He was playing in the last fixture of the 1958–59 season against Prahran, the club which produced Sam Loxton.

Owing to rain, no play was possible on the first day, Saturday, but on Monday North Melbourne gained an outright win by six wickets. The scores were Prahran 53 and 13; North Melbourne 52 and 15 for four wickets. In Prahran's first innings Jinkins took six wickets for 25 runs in eleven overs and in the second innings his analysis was eight wickets for no runs in 4.2 overs, a performance probably without parallel in senior cricket.

ESSEX v WARWICKSHIRE
Clacton, August 4, 5, 6, 1965

With Webster unable to bowl, A. C. Smith, the wicket-keeper, joined the attack and he performed the hat-trick at the expense of Barker, G. Smith and Fletcher. When disposing of Bailey, Smith had taken four wickets in 34 deliveries without cost, but grim defence saved Essex.

TWO TIMES TEN
[1989]

Andy Langston, an opening bowler for the Alexandra Park club in North London, performed a remarkable double feat inside one week in June 1988. On June 18, playing for Buckingham Palace, his former employer, he took all ten wickets for 59 in 20.3 overs against the Royal Household at Windsor Great Park. Five days later, on June 23, playing for Alexandra Park in a match celebrating their centenary, he took all ten wickets for 77 in 25.1 overs against a Club Cricket Conference President's XI.

PUNJAB v BARODA
Baroda, March 4, 5, 6, 7, 1999

Punjab's Harman Harry – aged 14 years 183 days – took a wicket with his first ball on first-class debut.

CRICKET IN MALTA
[1999]

Walter Glynn claimed a possible world record for international cricket when he appeared for Malta against Switzerland in the ECC

Tournament, aged 65. Glynn, who is of Maltese parentage, though his ancestors were British, bowls donkey drops from a yard behind the crease.

SRI LANKA v WEST INDIES
Kandy, November 21, 22, 23, 24, 25, 2001

The match had a bizarre start, when its fifth over was completed by three bowlers. Dillon had trapped Atapattu in his first over, but then, feeling unwell, left the field after two balls of his third. Stuart was asked to finish the over but sent down two unintentional head-high full tosses in three balls to Jayasuriya. Under ICC regulations, umpire Hampshire had no alternative but to direct the captain to remove him for the rest of the innings, the first instance of its kind in Test cricket. Gayle then bowled the last three balls of the over.

OXFORD UCCE v GLOUCESTERSHIRE
Oxford, April 9, 10, 11, 2005

After missing out on batting practice on the first day, Spearman gorged himself second time round with his third double-hundred in ten months: 216 in 168 balls and 254 minutes, with 23 fours and seven sixes, including 34 runs off debutant leg-spinner Stephen Moreton. It was 20-year-old Moreton's first over in first-class cricket, the last over of the second day, and it went for 666646. It was the worst start to a bowling career in first-class history: the Worcestershire wicketkeeper Steve Rhodes conceded 30 when he bowled against Somerset in 1991, but his team were hoping for a declaration – and the over included a no-ball. When Moreton came on, Spearman warned wicketkeeper Josh Knappett that he was going to swing at everything, and he kept his word. The first four balls were respectable leg-breaks but Spearman connected with them all. 'I was a bit concerned about six sixes,' Moreton said, 'so I tried a quicker ball for the fifth. It was such a rank long-hop, he miscued it so it only went for four.' He went on to play for Warwickshire Second Eleven, without similar disasters.

Packet of Matches

SIXTEEN OF THE COUNTRY ROUND
SHEFFIELD v SIXTEEN OF SHEFFIELD

On the Hyde Park Ground at Sheffield, August 13, 1838 (16 a side). Each player was sixty years of age, or upwards. The united ages of the Country side was 1010, and the Town side 1026.

2nd ROYAL SURREY MILITIA v SHILLINGLEE

The following extraordinary coincidence of getting eleven players out without scoring occurred at Shillinglee Park, Sussex, the seat of the Earl of Winterton, August 13, 1855:

2nd Royal Surrey Militia

Private Dudley b Challen, jun.	0	c Sadler b Challen jr 7
Private Plumbridge b Heather	0	b Randall 0
E. Hartnell Esq. b Heather	0	run out 15
A. Marshall Esq. b Challen jun.	0	b Randall 23
Private Ayling b Challen jun.	0	not out 9
Lieut Pontifex b Heather	0	b Challen jun. 6
Corporal Heyes b Heather	0	c Challen jun. b Randall .. 10
Lieut Ball b Heather	0	b Heather 0
Major Ridley not out	0	run out 0
Sergeant Ayling run out	0	c Sadler b Piggott 1
Private Newberry b Heather	0	b Heather 14
Extra	<u>0</u>	B 5, w 15, n-b 1 ...... <u>21</u>
	0	106

THE DREADED CYPHER
[1971]

Basil Easterbrook writes: It was No. 10 who nearly ruined the whole thing. He hit one to cover point and set off like an Olympic sprinter going for the tape. Major Ridley rent the pastoral scene with a stentorian voice of command—'Go Back Sergeant.' Sgt. Ayling pulled up all standing, fell base over apex and was run out by 15 yards. There were those who accused the gallant Major of moral cowardice, but I see him as a man with a sense of history. There is something aesthetically perfect about that scorecard—no catches, no stumping, no LBW's and no runs.

GRACE AND TARRANT v ELEVEN OF OTAGO
Dunedin, February 15, 1864

The Two

E. M. Grace lbw b Wills 7   – b Wills 10

G. Tarrant c Murison b Wills 1   – lbw b Wills 6

                                                              8   16

The Eleven

McDonald b Tarrant 0

Winter b Tarrant 0

Jacomb b Tarrant 0

Redfern b Tarrant 0

Wills c and b Tarrant 1

Worthington b Tarrant 1

Smith b Tarrant 0

Murison b Tarrant 1

Hamilton b Tarrant 0

Lamont b Tarrant 3

Thomas b Tarrant 1

                                                                                         7

The Eleven did not play their second innings.

ENGLAND v CASTLEMAINE

After the Castlemaine match, 1864, the following Single Wicket Match was played, Tarrant fielding for the two. England won by 12 runs.

England

E. M. Grace c Smith b Crawshaw	13
J. Jackson b Crawshaw	0
N-b 1	1
	14

Castlemaine

Amos b Jackson	1
Lewis b Jackson	0
Easton b Jackson	0
Wilson b Jackson	0
Govett b Jackson	0
Morris b Jackson	0
Crawshaw b Jackson	0
Smith b Jackson	0
Dow hit wkt b Jackson	1
Bond b Jackson	0
B. Butterworth hit wkt b Jackson	0
	2

RESULTS OF SINGLE v MARRIED OF ENGLAND MATCHES

At Tunbridge Wells, 1844. The Married won by 9 runs.

At Lord's, 1849. The Single won by three wickets.

At The Oval, 1858. The Single won by 16 runs.

At Lord's, 1871. The Single won as above.

ONE LEG v ONE ARM
Islington, April 22, 23, 1867

One Leg

Randall b Aldridge	1	– b Redfern	3
Murphy run out	0	– b Neal	0
Birchmore c and b Aldridge	46	– b Neal	62
W. Hammond b Aldridge	3	– b Neal	1
Wells b Neal	11	– b Neal	4
W. Brett b Neal	3	– c Worsam b Neal	28
Crabtree c Worsam b Neal	5	– c Worsam b Redfern	0
Barrs c Worsam b Aldridge	8	– c Worsam b Redfern	5
Hackley b Aldridge	5	– b Redfern	4
Butler not out	0	– b Redfern	0
Oliver b Neal	1	– c Worsam b Neal	0
Heath b Aldridge	0	– not out	15
B 1, l-b 5	6	B 5, w 5	10
	89		132

One Arm

R. Smith c Birchmore b Barrs	12	– b Brett	11
W. S. Smith run out	2	– not out	0
B. Neal b Crabtree	12	– b Brett	5
Redfern not out	59	– b Birchmore	9
Aldridge b Crabtree	26	– c and b Crabtree	3
Gurney b Crabtree	4	– b Crabtree	2
Boucher b Wells	5	– c Hackley b Crabtree	7
Hindley b Weels	0		
Worsam b Crabtree	8	– b Crabtree	16
M'Crossen b Wells	5	– b Brett	1
Hines b Butler	1		
Harris b Butler	0	– b Crabtree	2
B 8, w 1	9	B 1, l-b 1, n-b 1	3
	143		59

RIGHT HANDED v LEFT HANDED OF ENGLAND
Lord's, May 9, 10, 1870

This was the opening match of the 84th season of The Marylebone Club. So brilliant an array of the cricketing talent of the country on no prior occasion appeared in an opening match at Lord's, the match being moreover interesting from its not having been played since 1835, and for its being the first match Carpenter, Hayward, and Smith had played in at Lord's since 1866. The weather was bright, but nippingly cold for May.

THE AMERICAN BASE BALL PLAYERS IN ENGLAND
[1874]

Twenty-two base ball players from America visited England at the back end of the cricket season, 1874, 'their mission' – it was semi-officially stated – 'being to give the English a practical insight into the workings of base ball.' The twenty-two comprised eleven members of the Boston (red stockings) and eleven of the Philadelphia Athletes (blue stockings), the two leading base ball clubs in the United States, where the game holds the same high and popular national position cricket does in England. The visitors' stay in this country was limited to one month. They quickly got to work, making their first appearance in flannel on an English ground the 30th of July, at Edgehill, the ground of the Liverpool Cricket Club. They were a finely-framed, powerful set of men and, although 'Base Ball' did not take the popular fancy here, the splendid long-distance throwing and truly magnificent out-fielding of the Americans at once won the full and heartily-expressed admiration of Englishmen, who frankly and freely acknowledged the Americans' superiority to the generality of English fielders.

THE AMERICANS AT LORD'S

Considerable interest was excited in cricketing circles last summer by public announcements that representative teams of the two leading Base Ball Clubs of America would, at the back end of our cricket season visit England and by playing their national game on our principal

cricket grounds, endeavour to acclimatise that game in this country. The interest created by this announcement was increased by the statement that the Americans had also (but somewhat reluctantly) agreed to play a cricket match against an English Club team on each ground they played their base ball match on.

12 GENTLEMEN OF MCC v 18 OF AMERICA

The MCC batting was commenced by Mr Alfred Lubbock and Mr Courtenay, to the bowling of H. Wright (medium round) and McBride (fast underhand) who took three strides to the wicket and then let fly a tremendously fast grubber that rarely rose from the ground an inch after it pitched; this kind of bowling quickly settled Mr Courtenay and Mr Round and at first somewhat stuck up Mr Alfred Lubbock, who, however, soon got into something like his old fine form of play, scored 24 runs, and was then clean bowled by H. Wright. Mr Lubbock left with the score at 34 and at 41 a clever catch at point settled Mr Lucas for 12. One more run was scored and then – at five minutes past two – they retired to luncheon and preparations were forthwith made for commencing:

THE BASE BALL MATCH
ATHLETIC CLUB 9 v BOSTON CLUB 9

The Boston men were the Base Ball champions of America and The Athletics (of Philadelphia) the ex-champions. The marking out the diamond-shaped base ground, and the subsequent play of the sides was watched with marked interest by the audience, but they had not proceeded far with the match before many of the spectators were impressed with the idea that they were witnessing a modernised, manly – and unquestionably an improved – edition of that most enjoyable old game of their boyhood — Rounders, the most patent differences being: – a cricket-sized ball is used at base ball, instead of a ball of tennis size, as at rounders; throwing the ball at the striker when running from base to base is allowed at rounders, but is properly barred at base ball; and instead of the ball being struck with a stick of broom-handle thickness held in one hand, as at rounders, it is at base ball struck by a formidably-sized club, clutched and wielded by both hands, a form of play that, to become efficient in, evidently requires lengthened practice and much skill.

The play proceeded to the evident advantage of the Bostonians all through; and after a contest of two hours and ten minutes' duration, the Boston Champions won by 27 to 7.

Play in the cricket match was resumed at 6 o'clock, Mr V. E. Walker and Mr Bird continuing the MCC batting. Mr V. E. Walker hit freely and got well hold of the bowling, but was at last settled by a good ball from H. Wright and was out for 27 – the highest score hit in the match. Then play ceased for the day, the MCC score standing at 88 for five wickets, Mr Bird not out, 15. The Americans fielded very smartly and effectively before luncheon, but subsequent to their base ball struggle their fielding was loose and ineffective.

BATS v BROOMSTICKS

The abrupt and early termination of the match on August 15, 1877, was the cause of a fill-up-the-time match being arranged for the Gloucestershire Eleven with broomsticks, to play Eleven of Cheltenham with bats. The broomsticks made a first innings of 290 runs; of those runs

Dr E. M. Grace made 103, and Midwinter 58.

The batsmen had lost two wickets and scored 50 runs, when time was up.

HUNTSMEN OF ENGLAND v JOCKEYS
Lord's, May 29, 1880

MCC AND GROUND v FIFTEEN CANADIANS
Lord's, June 10, 1880

If fifty Canadians of the calibre of this fifteen had been brought into the field it is possible, even probable, that MCC would still have been victorious, so miserable was the display made by the visitors. H.

Lemmon, who scored 14 not out, and G. E. Hall, 13, were the only two who managed to reach double figures, while no less than six of the Canadians figured with 'a pair of them'.

SMOKERS v NON-SMOKERS
Lord's, September 15, 16, 1884
This match was played for the benefit of the Cricketers' Fund Friendly Society, and, contrary to the anticipations of many, proved one of the most attractive contests of the season.

GOVERNMENT v OPPOSITION
Lord's, July 29, 1893
A match between members of Parliament representing respectively the Government and Opposition was played, but did not prove the attraction expected.

HIGHBURY PARK SCHOOL v ISLINGTON HIGH SCHOOL
Muswell Hill, June 12, 1897
The score of this match is published as a curiosity, the losers being dismissed without getting a run and second innings for five, a total of 21 proving sufficient to win the game by an innings and 16 runs. Wiggins took eleven wickets for two runs.

Highbury Park School

Innes b Jones	3
Haslett b Fairman	4
L. Jones b Fairman	3
Wiggins c Bartram b Fairman	2
C. Buckney c Taylor b Jones	4
Wright b Fairman	2
Masters run out	1
A. Vasey not out	0
Poulton b Fairman	0

Kirby b Fairman I
W. Reid c Rilerosthy b Fairman .... o
   B I 1

                                                           21

Islington High School

	1st innings		2nd innings	
Fairman c Haslett b Wiggins	o	b Wiggins	o
Staley b Jones	o	b Jones	o
Bull c Haslett b Jones	o	b Jones	o
Bartram b Wiggins	o	b Wiggins	o
Rilerosthy b Wiggins	o	c Wiggins b James	o
Cook b Wiggins	o	not out	o
Gardner b Jones	o	c Innes b Wiggins	2
Taylor run out	o	b Wiggins	2
C. Jones not out	o	b Wiggins	o
Dunn b Wiggins	o	c Haslett b Wiggins	1
	o		**5**

UNDER THIRTY-TWO v OVER THIRTY-TWO
Hastings, September 6, 7, 8, 1950

IRELAND v WEST INDIES
Sion Mills, Londonderry, July 2, 1969

Ireland won by nine wickets. In some ways this one-day match provided the sensation of the 1969 season. The West Indies, with six of the team who had escaped on the previous day from defeat in the Lord's Test, were skittled for 25 in this tiny Ulster town on a damp and definitely emerald green pitch. The conditions were all in favour of the bowlers, but the West Indies batsmen fell in the main to careless strokes and smart catching. Goodwin, the Irish captain, took five wickets for 6 runs and O'Riordan four for 18. Both bowled medium pace at a reasonable length and the pitch did the rest.

Crowds and Critics

NORTH v SOUTH
Lord's, June 10, 11 and 12, 1878

The people thronged the Grand Stand – they crowded to inconvenience the players' seats at the north end of the pavilion – they filled to an inch the embankment seats at the NE and SW corners – they completely blocked up the Tavern steps – they sat as closely together as they could sit on the garden wall tops – every window looking on the ground was filled with lookers on, and not only did the visitors stand five or six deep behind the ring, but at top and bottom of the ground, they swarmed in hundreds before the ring, thereby materially contracting the fielding space and rendering 'hits to the people' not worth more than half the runs they were booked for. But for all that, the 10,000 present were, as a rule, a jolly and good tempered crowd; and when Mr W. G. Grace went to and entreated them, in his well known bland and courteous manner, to get back a bit and give a little more fielding space, they laughed at, chaffed and shook hands with the crack in the most enjoyable, merry and free and easy form; and by this and other ways practically proved that 'the enlightened foreigner' who wrote 'the English took their pleasures churlishly', knew nothing about the matter, and wrote a famous fib.

SOUTH AFRICANS v SUSSEX
Brighton, July 2, 3, 1894

The game failed entirely to attract the Brighton public.

GLOUCESTERSHIRE v SUSSEX
Bristol, August 6, 7, 8, 1894

Owing to unfavourable weather the game could not be commenced on Monday, and an unpleasant episode occurred. Drenching rains on Sunday had left the ground very heavy, there was a further downpour on Monday, and at three o'clock, the umpires declaring the turf quite unfit for cricket, it was decided to postpone the start. In the meantime, however, some two or three thousand spectators had been admitted to the ground, and, on learning the decision, they behaved in a very unsportsmanlike manner. A number of them trampled on the playing portion of the ground, doing considerable damage, and Mr W. G. Grace and Mr Murdoch, the captains, were mobbed and had to be protected by the police. This regrettable incident points to the necessity of gate money not being taken until play has been definitely decided upon.

YORKSHIRE v AN ENGLAND ELEVEN
Scarborough, September 5, 6, 1895

A very disagreeable incident marred the pleasure of a game that presented few features of interest. Owing to the state of the ground a start could not be made at the ordinary time on the first day, and a section of the crowd indulged in a most unseemly demonstration, such insulting remarks being addressed to Mr H. T. Hewett that that gentleman – who was to have captained the England team – retired from the match after fielding till the luncheon interval. We think he acted unwisely, but he was much provoked.

AUSTRALIANS v MIDDLESEX
Lord's, August 21, 22, 1899

On the first day the game was marred by an unseemly demonstration on the part of spectators, happily without precedent at Lord's. Resenting the extreme caution with which Darling and Iredale were batting, a section of the crowd forgot their manners, cheering ironically when a run was obtained, and at one point whistling the 'Dead March in Saul'.

NOTES BY THE EDITOR, 1920

It is to be feared that a good many people who find their pleasure in watching cricket are very ignorant of the game. In no other way can one account for the unseemly 'barracking' that sometimes goes on. A particularly bad case occurred in the Middlesex and Yorkshire match at Lord's in August. J. W. Hearne, playing as well as he has ever played in his life, was doing his utmost to save Middlesex from defeat and yet a section of the crowd hooted him. A remedy for this sort of nuisance is not easy to find, as obviously the batsman cannot leave the wickets. A stoppage of the game, however, with all the players staying on the field, might have the effect of bringing the malcontents to their senses.

ENGLAND v AUSTRALIA
Lord's, May 29, 1944

Roper lacked control of length and direction; possibly unseemly hand-clapping as he moved to his starting place affected a sensitive temperament.

WEST INDIES v ENGLAND
Georgetown, February 24, 25, 26, 27, March 1, 2, 1954

Apparently disagreeing with the decision of Menzies, the umpire and groundsman, sections of the crowd hurled bottles and wooden packing-cases on to the field and some of the players were fortunate to escape injury. The President of the British Guiana Cricket Association went out and suggested to Hutton that the players should leave but Hutton preferred to remain. He wanted more wickets. His was a courageous action for which he deserved much praise. In the last over England took another wicket and early on the fifth day they enforced the follow-on.

WEST INDIES v ENGLAND
Port-of-Spain, January 28, 29, 30, February 1, 2, 3, 1960

Excitement was intense throughout and it led to an unfortunate and remarkable scene on the third day. A crowd of almost 30,000, a record for any sporting event in West Indies, became so inflamed that soon after tea tempers boiled over and a few hooligans began throwing bottles on to the outfield. This started an orgy of bottle-throwing and a large part of the crowd wandered on to the playing area. Things became so bad that a riot developed. The England players were escorted from the field, though no animosity was being shown to them. No further play was possible that day. Bottles were also thrown at Georgetown on the previous MCC tour six years earlier but on that occasion the cricket was resumed after a short delay. During the match players on both sides were told to play their parts in avoiding incidents by accepting umpiring decisions without quibble and by walking immediately they were given out.

INDIA v ENGLAND
Kanpur, December 1, 2, 3, 5, 6, 1961

Numerous stoppages occurred during the match, largely because spectators flashed mirrors and biscuit tins in the eyes of the batsmen. Missiles were thrown at fieldsmen and fights and fires frequently broke out, the crowd being unruly throughout.

INDIA v WEST INDIES
Calcutta, December 31, 1967, January 1, 3, 4, 5, 1968

This match will find a place in the history of Test cricket not because of the cricket it produced, but because of the horrible riot that broke out on the second day. The authorities had sold more tickets than there were seats and inevitably the surplus spectators tried to find accommodation on the grass round the boundaries. The constabulary mounted a baton charge, the crowd launched a counter-attack and when the outnumbered police force fled, the crowd burnt down the stands and furniture.

It was indeed a frightening scene and the players, worried about their safety, were reluctant to continue the match, which came pretty close to being abandoned till assurances were received from high governmental quarters that there would be no further incidents.

INDIA v NEW ZEALAND
Hyderabad, October 15, 16, 18, 19, 20, 1969

Venkataraghavan and Bedi, with 40 for the last wicket, batted bravely, but a youth, coming on to the field to congratulate the batsmen, was injured by a soldier and this incident provoked an ugly riot, in which gates were broken down, metal chairs flung on to the ground, fires lit in the stands, and the crowd attacked by an army unit. No play was possible in the last half-hour.

Dowling batted four hours, ten minutes for 60 but progress was slow, the Indian bowling rate dropping badly. New Zealand declared at the end of the fourth day, India thus having five and a half hours to score 268. Again the New Zealand pace bowlers were completely on top and the seventh wicket fell at 66. Over two and a quarter hours of playing time remained when the rain clouds burst, and there was a very heavy fall for half an hour, followed by hot sunshine. No real effort was made to get play started again. Instead of the covers being removed, a few workers with rags, some of them women, were given the task of removing the water from the covers and although there were official denials later, it looked very much like a deliberate go-slow policy. For perhaps the first time in cricket history a Test captain (Dowling) was on the field in bare feet, helping to remove the water. The match was abandoned twenty minutes before time, and this brought another demonstration by the crowd.

NORTH-EASTERN TRANSVAAL v AUSTRALIANS
Pretoria, January 6, 7, 8, 1970

No coloured-skin people were permitted to attend.

SOMERSET v WORCESTERSHIRE
Weston-super-Mare, August, 5, 6, 7, 1970

With four hours left to play, and the pitch quickly returning to placidity, neither side made any apparent effort to provide an interesting finish. Towards the end a small section of a considerable holiday crowd who were watching in glorious weather, peacefully demonstrated their resentment at the players' refusal even to offer a gesture towards entertaining them.

A BLOW ON THE BOX
[1984]

A protest group in Pakistan attempted unsuccessfully to have cricket banned from television, claiming that attendances at mosques fell away sharply when the Test series between Pakistan and India was being televised. A spokesman for the group, which petitioned the President, asserted that the media's main purpose should be 'to implement and propagate Islam and not give mileage to a game more British than Asian'.

A CASE FOR CORNHILL
[1984]

A woman walked on to the County Ground at Southampton last season to demand an apology from Robin Smith, who, while batting for Hampshire Second XI, had hit a ball through a window of her flat. Mrs Iris Clarke, aged 62, refused to return the ball. Hampshire, in their turn, advised her to refer the matter to her insurance company.

PAKISTAN v SRI LANKA
Hyderabad, November 3, 1985

Madugalle, who was fielding at third man, was injured when he was hit by a stone thrown from the stands.

PAKISTAN v WEST INDIES
Sialkot, November 14, 1986

Prior to the start, a crowd of some 5,000 outside the ground, unable to join the 25,000 already inside, was shelled with teargas canisters and many were injured in the stampede that followed. In another incident, five people suffered broken limbs when the branch of a tree gave way under the weight of watchers.

HAMPSHIRE v MIDDLESEX
Bournemouth, August 18, 19, 20, 1992

Hampshire's hopes of marking their final first-class match at Dean Park with a win were dashed by some obdurate Middlesex batting. After the game, a spectator placed a solitary rose on the wicket with a card marked, 'Fondest Memories of Hampshire cricket at Bournemouth – Will Ye No Come Back Again?'

INDIA v ENGLAND
Chandigarh, January 21, 1993

Chaotic crowd control resulted in a fatal shooting. Nearly 10,000 people attempted to force their way into the Sector 16 Stadium, already jam-packed to its 25,000 capacity, and as a path was being cleared for the Governor of Punjab, a pistol shot wounded two policemen, one of whom later died in hospital.

PAKISTAN v AUSTRALIA
Gujranwala, October 26, 1994

Rain forced officials to call off the game but, fearing for their safety when the large crowd rioted, they persuaded the teams to play a 12-a-side exhibition match of 15 overs an innings. The deputy commissioner of Gujranwala told Taylor, the Australian captain, 'If you don't play some cricket they'll kill us.' Taylor said he had never heard a more pressing reason to play. About sixty people were hurt in the disturbances. Conditions were so damp that bowling was possible only from one end; Pakistan reversed their batting order and won by four wickets.

CAMBRIDGE UNIVERSITY v GLAMORGAN
Cambridge, April 17, 18, 19, 1996

The unluckiest participant was Watkin who had his wallet stolen. He asked a member of the press to cancel his credit cards for him while he was in the field, leading to the unusual shout of 'Bowler's mother's maiden name'.

DERBYSHIRE v LEICESTERSHIRE
Derby, May 5, 1996

At the ball of Barnett's wicket, a bogus batsman in Derbyshire replica kit made his way to the crease, along with a startled Adams. The intruder was allowed to face a joke delivery before being hustled away.

AUSTRALIA v SOUTH AFRICA
Sydney, December 4, 1997

South African captain Cronje threatened to take his side off the field after Symcox was pelted with golf balls, fruit and a stuffed barbecued chicken from the boundary.

WEST INDIES v AUSTRALIA
Kingston, March 13, 14, 15, 16, 1999

Lara was circumspect early on, but stepped up a gear to strike MacGill for two sixes in an over, and Blewett for four successive fours. He drove Warne for a third six, and hit 28 fours in all, batting for 469 minutes and 344 balls. It was his 11th century in Tests – but the first since June 1997 – and his third double. He gave a chance on 44, off McGrath, when Mark Waugh dropped him at slip, and could have been run out for 99 when Blewett demolished the stumps. The crowd decided he had safely completed a cheeky single before the third umpire delivered his verdict, which might have included an element of benefit of the doubt; only one camera was available. Lara had to be rescued by security men from the enveloping throng and then awaited the verdict on the boundary. No one knows how

Sabina might have responded had he been given out. His double-century came without the same uncertainty but was greeted even more rapturously; one man ran on with a baby in his arms; another wore only a bandanna on his head. Lara sensibly retreated to the pavilion.

AUSTRALIA v PAKISTAN
Lord's, June 20, 1999

Lord's was awash with disinterested observers, while from outside came the klaxon, whistle and bugle of fanatical Pakistan support. About a hundred fans clambered up a building site overlooking the ground. As the police moved in, a game of cat and mouse ensued, providing an alternative spectacle for the Grand Stand opposite. Eventually, the fans, like their team, were unceremoniously bundled out of St John's Wood.

ORISSA v MADHYA PRADESH
Gwalior, March 22, 23, 24, 25, 26, 2001

Play was held up for 38 minutes on the fourth day after journalists invaded the pitch to demand an apology from Hirwani and Yadav who, they claimed, had manhandled one of their colleagues.

ESSEX v SURREY
Ilford, June 13, 14, 15, 15, 2001

The opening day had seen two miscreants entering Valentines Park: in one incident, a joyrider, after crashing a car near by, made his getaway through the park; in another, groundstaff discovered a man dangling from the railings, having tried to evade the admission fee.

NEW ZEALAND v ENGLAND
Wellington, February 16, 2002

Hussain later pointed to a lack of intensity. The crowd had no such problems, particularly during the interval, when Peter Jackson, the director of *The Lord of the Rings*, stood on the pitch with a microphone and persuaded them to make howling, growling, grunting noises for use in battle scenes in *The Two Towers*.

SRI LANKA v ENGLAND
Colombo, December 18, 19, 20, 21, 2003

Outside the ground there was chaos too, as police prevented a group of Buddhist monks from storming the stadium. The monks were furious that the cricket had not been halted out of respect for a well-known colleague, the Venerable Gangodavila Soma Thera, who had died the previous week.

INDIA v SOUTH AFRICA
Kanpur, November 20, 21, 22, 23, 24, 2004

With the match dribbling to a draw, a TV cameraman spotted a young man sitting near the boundary, cradling a .38 calibre revolver. When he was apprehended, the authorities were embarrassed to discover he was Taslimuddin Pasha, son of the president of the Kanpur Cricket Association, and had been granted an access-all-areas pass. His intentions remained unclear – he claimed carrying a gun was simply the done thing in that part of the world – but police confirmed he had breached ground regulations by bringing in a firearm. It provided a late frisson in a game that neither Sehwag's ebullience nor Hall's obduracy could raise from a morass of mediocrity.

YORKSHIRE v WARWICKSHIRE
Scarborough, July 24, 2005

Just before the end, a spectator wearing an Osama bin Laden mask and with a rucksack on his back ran on to the field; he was ejected from the ground.

2011 WORLD CUP QUALIFYING SERIES

Long before the 2007 World Cup got under way, qualifying began for the 2011 tournament. Norway, comprising Norwegian-born players of Pakistani ancestry, had emerged from the nine-team European Third Division field in Belgium to proceed, along with Greece, to the second-tier tournament in Scotland. Norway duly won that too, beating Associate-member opposition five times, all by substantial margins.

In Scotland, conditions for Norway's match against Israel at New Anniesland in Glasgow were less than idyllic. Due to about a hundred demonstrators protesting against the Israeli invasion of Lebanon, both teams' coaches came with police escorts, the match continuing as helicopters flew overhead. Israel's match against Jersey was abandoned altogether because the only 'secure' playing venue had been booked for a children's playgroup. Their match against Guernsey, due to have been played in Glasgow, was switched to the Royal Air Force base at Lossiemouth, 150 miles away.

Related and Not

ALFRED JOHN ATFIELD
(1868–1949)

A member of the ground staff at Lord's from 1901, he scored 121 not out on that ground in a Cross Arrows match after his marriage earlier in the day at Hanover Square.

SURREY v MIDDLESEX
The Oval, June 15, 16, 1891

Probably the best display of batting in the match was given by Mr T. C. O'Brien, who, at this period of the season, was playing under the name of J. E. Johnston.

DERBYSHIRE v WARWICKSHIRE
Derby, June 3, 5, 1922

At one time the two Quaifes were opposed by the two Bestwicks. For father and son to be batting against bowlers similarly related was a remarkable incident – regarded as unique in county cricket.

MIDDLESEX v SOMERSET
Lord's, 22, 23, 24 June, 1933

H. W. Lee c F. S. Lee b J. W. Lee …… 82 — run out …… 14

MCC v NEW SOUTH WALES COUNTRY
Newcastle, November 17, 18, 1950

Berry and Brown spun out the local side, but MCC shaped poorly against medium-paced bowling. Their main troubles were caused by one John Bull. The pill tasted no less bitter because of that.

JAMES GRAHAM BINKS [b 1935]

His father, Jim, was a keen cricketer and kept wicket for the G.P.O. and Hull 2nd XI. His fingers were gnarled and mis-shapen. He stood up to the stumps for every bowler, suffered many injuries, and for this reason wanted his son to be a bowler. But the son wanted to be like father.

SUNIL MANOHAR GAVASKAR (b 1949)

He was born with the scent of bat oil in his nostrils, for his father was still a very active club cricketer and his uncle from his mother's side, M. K. Mantri, was Bombay's and India's wicket-keeper. In the circumstances, it was no surprise that a toy cricket bat was among his earliest possessions, and that the infant Gavaskar's afternoon naps were followed by practice against the bowling of a doting mother and the houseboy. The most prolific Indian batsman ever in Test cricket says that he learnt to read numbers from scoreboards.

SIDATH WETTIMUNY (b 1956)

He was the third son of an engineer. The eldest son, Sunil, opened the batting for Sri Lanka in pre-Test days; the second son, Mithra, played two Tests as Sidath's opening partner early in 1983, the first instance of two brothers opening a Test innings since W. G. and E. M. Grace in 1880. They all attended Ananda College, the leading Buddhist school in Colombo, and progressed through the schoolboy competitions which give the island's cricket so much of its strength.

However, Ramsey Wettimuny, father of the household, may have had the decisive impact on his sons. He became chief engineer of the Ceylon Transport Board and visited England, where he was attracted to cricket for the first time and also – being technically minded – to the works of C. B. Fry. Indeed, he read Fry's *Batsmanship* (1912) so often that a typed copy of it had to be made. Then he built an indoor cricket school, which Sidath claims to have been the first in Sri Lanka, and there inculcated in his sons the principles of batsmanship as expounded by Fry.

Wettimuny remembers in particular the chapter on wristwork: 'When we cannot quite explain something in a stroke we refer it to the wrists, or else to timing; and end by vouchsafing the information that timing is largely a matter of wrists.' But Fry goes on to analyse the subject in scientific detail, using terms like 'longitudinal arm-turn'. All this impressed the young Sidath: and those cuts and cover drives he produced at Lord's owed much to the last-second flick of the left wrist which Fry prescribes as the source of proper timing.

OXFORD UNIVERSITY v CAMBRIDGE UNIVERSITY
June 26, 28, 29, 1982

John Varey, bowling for Oxford, gave the 1982 match another place in history by taking the wicket of his twin brother, David.

AUSTRALIA v INDIA
Sydney, January 2, 3, 4, 5, 6, 1986

Just 54 runs were required to save the follow-on, but on the final morning Border holed out to long-on. His concentration may have wavered because his wife, at the time, was in labour in a Brisbane hospital. By the time the new Border had arrived, Australia were following on. Matthews, who had helped Border check the collapse on the fourth day, was also out to an injudicious stroke, and the last five wickets fell for just 9 runs.

WARWICKSHIRE v GLAMORGAN
Birmingham, July 30, 31, August 1, 2, 1998

Both sides fielded a Michael J. Powell.

DENIS COMPTON SCHOLAR

The Compton Scholar is the overall winner of an award given to the most promising player at each county, organised by NBC Sports Management since 1997. The winner in 2006 was Nick Compton of Middlesex.

Victoriana

MCC AND GROUND v THE COUNTY OF HERTFORDSHIRE
Chorleywood, June 11, 12, 1869

For the score of this match the compiler is indebted to a report in *Bell's Life in London*, a most lucid, crisp, and compact cricket report, that commented on 'King Charles the Second and Nell Gwynne; Macauley; The Evangelization of the Heathen; Mary-la-Bonne; War paint; A Straight Derby Tip; Knaves of Herts; Small Boys; A County Policeman and Stricken Herts.'

ETON v HARROW
Lord's, July 9, 10, 1869

That this, the most attractive match of the season, annually increases in popularity with the fair and fashionable portion of English society Lord's ground bore brilliant testimony on Friday, the 9th of last July, on which day £100 more was taken at the gates for admission than was ever before taken in one day at Lord's. The weather was fortunately fine; the attendance marvellous, both in numbers and quality; and the old ground, as it that day appeared, a fitting subject for a companion picture to Frith's 'Derby Day'. One writer described the Grand Stand as being 'as gay as a bank of Summer Flowers', and so it was, for two-thirds of the occupants were 'The Ladies of England', whose gay, varied, and brilliant hued attires pleasantly contrasted with the dark, sombre clad, dense mass of 'he' humanity that thronged the seats and roof of the Pavilion, a majority of whom 'had been' Public School Boys, many of whom 'are' distinguished members of the highest and most honoured Institutions of the Country. As many of the Drags of 'The Four-in-Hand Club' as could gain admission to the ground were grouped together at the NW end of the Pavilion. Around the ground flanking the ropes, closely clustered (at most parts six deep) were 600 carriages of the nobility and gentry, each vehicle fully, most of them 'fairly' freighted.

JOHN MAUDE
(1850–1934)

Going to Eton when 10 as a colleger he was there for nine years under three headmasters—Goodford, Balston, and Hornby. His tutor was the Rev. J. E. Yonge. In his time he had three future Bishops as fags— Welldon (Calcutta), Ryle (Liverpool) and Harmer (Rochester).

In 1869 Maude, by taking seven wickets for 36 in the second innings, contributed largely to Eton's victory by an innings and 19 runs. Of that famous match Mr. H. S. Salt, in his 'Memories of Bygone Eton', wrote: 'C. J. Ottaway made a century. Thanks mainly to his patient and skilful batting and to some fine left-hand bowling by John Maude, the match ended in a single innings victory for Eton. Old Stephen Hawtrey is said to have stopped Maude in the street and asked to be allowed to shake "that noble hand," which by a wonderful "caught and bowled" had disposed of Harrow's most formidable batsman. We all believed the story. It seemed exactly what Stephen Hawtrey would have done. But 57 years later I was told by Maude that he had no recollection of the incident. It *ought* to have happened, anyhow.'

ETON v HARROW
Lord's, July 8, 9, 1870

Their Royal Highnesses the Duchess of Cambridge and the Prince and Princess of Teck, with a host of the nobility, honoured this match with their presence at Lord's. The Grand Stand was thronged, a large majority of its occupants being ladies. The Pavilion seats and roof were crowded with members and their friends. 'The Ring' was deeper and more densely packed and the outer ring of carriages more extensive than at any preceding match. Such an assemblage of rank, fashion and numbers had never before been seen even at Lord's. It was computed that quite 30,000 visitors attended the ground on those memorable two days. Two sights unusual on cricket grounds and curious by contrast, were witnessed at this match: the first occurred on the Friday, when on the 'boys' retiring to luncheon the whole playing area of the ground was

covered by a gay company promenading; the other on the Saturday, when on rain commencing falling at noon the youthful cricketers were suddenly surrounded by a dense ring of some thousands of opened umbrellas.

OXFORD v CAMBRIDGE
Lord's, June 25, 26, 1877

The innings over, the visitors crowded on to the playing portion of the ground in great numbers; in fact, Lord's ground was then literally covered by the fashionable throng. The gaily dressed ladies slowly promenading; the thickly packed crowd swaying to and fro in front of the Pavilion; the mass of people outside the ropes down at the bottom of the ground, perforce moving onwards at a snail's pace, and at times coming to a dead block, unable to move either way; and the chock at the top of the ground when the police mandate rang out, 'Clear the ground', 'Clear the ground there', 'Ladies, do pray clear the ground', formed a sight that those who were in a position to look down on never can forget, for truly said a 20-years' regular attendant at Lord's, 'It is a sight that never had an equal on a cricket-ground.' But at last the entreaties of the police cleared the ground sufficiently to finish off the match.

THE CANTERBURY WEEK
August 10, 1871

Thursday – The Ladies' Day – was one of those bright, cloudless, hot days, that in August last so frequently gladdened the hearts of farmers, tourists and pleasure-seekers. When the cricket commenced the company present hardly warranted expectations of an assemblage up to the usual Thursday magnitude, but from noon to four p.m. visitors arrived in large numbers. Four-in-hands skilfully tooled, old fashioned family carriages whisked along in the old fashioned 4-horse postillion form, new fashioned breaks and waggonettes, dashing dogcarts, tandems, 'busses and other vehicles, all of them fully, most of them fairly, freighted, rattled up the incline of the fine old ground one after the other in such numbers, that when the rush was over and all were settled in picturesque groups, when the little slope was covered by brightly toileted ladies, when the promenade was thronged by a gay company and when the ring around the ground was fully formed, it was unanimously acknowledged that the gathering was the gayest, the most numerous and influential ever seen at a cricket match at St. Lawrence. Truly was this 'The Ladies' Day,' for of the 7000 visitors present 'the better half' were ladies, whose presence so very much enhanced the beauty of that charming, animated picture of English summer life.

THE CANTERBURY WEEK
August 4, 5, 6, 7, 8, 9, 1873

The clerical, staid, quiet, quaint old 'City of the Men of Kent' was, from Monday morn until Saturday eve, dressed up in an unwonted gay form, the whole length of the ancient High Street being ablaze with flags: scarce a house in that long, narrow, and historically interesting thoroughfare but what had its bits of bunting blowing in the breeze, and at about every two score yards or so a string of flags of all colours streamed across the street. The Union Jack; the rampant White Horse of Kent; the famous old buff and blue of politics; the gorgeous red, black, and gold of 'I Zingari'; the sombre black and blue of Kent's 'Band of Brothers'; the scarlet and black of 'The Knickerbocker's'; the ever popular red and gold of MCC; the dark blue of Oxford; the light blue of Cambridge; the blue and yellow of the RA; and lots of other banners crowdedly covered the house fronts in the High Street, and as the strong wind fluttered them they seemed to cheerily wave welcomes to all comers to The Canterbury Week of 1873.

THE CANTERBURY WEEK
August 7, 8, 9, 10, 11, 12, 1876

The two County Balls appear to have been as numerously attended by the fair maids, matrons, and magnates of the county as heretofore; and 'The Old Stagers' drew to the little theatre as large, light-hearted, laughing audience as they ever attracted since 'the theatricals' of 'The O.S.' were first played in the old theatre in 1842.

'KENT AGAINST ALL THE WORLD'

An epilogue usually finishes up the dramatic performances of 'The Week'. In the epilogue spoken in the theatre on the conclusion of the 1877 performances Lord Harris had to utter his indignant protest against all 'obstructives', cricketing or otherwise; and thus his lordship spoke:

> 'Hold! I protest, for here I present
>   All – MCC, I Zingari and Kent.
> Ne'er shall such trivial, childish schemes be found
>   To desecrate our famed St. Lawrence Ground.
> There, let Kent's white-horse banner be unfurled
> Against All England – aye, 'gainst All The World.'

THE CANTERBURY WEEK AUGUST 1881

The 'Old Stagers' met with great success, the programme being 'The Charming Woman', 'Out of Light', 'Tit for Tat', 'A Thumping Legacy', and 'Hester's Mystery'. Lord Harris's absence was feelingly alluded to in the original epilogue, which concludes the Canterbury Week, in the following lines:

> 'Our pleasure's tainted by one heavy grief –
> The absence of our former cricket chief,
> For all the pluck with which he strove to raise
> Her cricket to the height of former days
> Kent owes to him – that is no empty platitude –
> A deep and everlasting debt of gratitude;

'Tis sad his dear familiar face to miss,
But we must consolation seek in this;
Though him and us a cruel distance parts,
We are in his as he in all our hearts.'

On Wednesday and Thursday the usual balls took place at the Freemasons' Hall, where dancing was kept up with great zeal to the strains of Gates's band.

The Greater Game

NORTHAMPTONSHIRE v LANCASHIRE
Northampton, 23, 24, 25 August 1939

W. H. Lister b Merritt . . . . <u>31</u> – absent . . . . <u>0</u>

In August 1939 Lionel Lister, Lancashire captain since 1936, was padded up at Northampton when he was summoned by his territorial regiment. He said goodbye to his team-mates, and never played another first-class match.

MR. BEVIN ORDERED CRICKET

Sir Pelham Warner told the Club Cricket Conference at their 1942 annual meeting that in July 1940 he was rung up by Mr. Ernest Bevin's secretary and asked to send a cricket team to the industrial North.

After Dunkirk, men and women had been working extremely hard. Mr. Bevin was anxious that some recreation should be provided for them, and they greatly enjoyed the game. War comes first, second and all the time, but cricket can take off some of the grimness. As Mr. Herbert Morrison reminded us recently, total war need not mean total misery.

Mr. Stanley Christopherson, MCC president, told the 300 club representatives that, following Dunkirk, 'An officer came to my box at Lord's haggard and tired and he remarked, "To see this green grass and the bat and ball is heaven!" When that officer left the ground his face had quite a different appearance.'

SUSSEX v AN R.A.F. XI
Lewes, May 18, 1940

In this match there appeared J. F. Boughey, who played for Sussex 2nd XI on several occasions in 1939. He was the Eton captain of 1938, and his death, a few weeks later, came as a great shock to all his friends in the Sussex club.

A MIDDLESEX XI v A LORD'S XI
Lord's, September 7, 1940

Middlesex XI won by 32 runs. This 'family affair' of colleagues at Headquarters came to a strange and dramatic end after a prolonged wait for 'All Clear'. Gray then dismissed Taylor and Major Cartwright with consecutive balls; a leg-bye from the next delivery was followed by Brooks being leg-before, while, after a single, the fast bowler finished the match a few minutes before time. The long delay essential under the Government regulations as to 'taking cover' during an air raid seemed to have made a draw inevitable, but the strict rule made by Headquarters to play out time if possible gave the opportunity which Gray seized so promptly.

ODDS AND ENDS
[1941]

A. T. C. Geary, the former Surrey cricketer, who for some seasons has acted as coach to Victoria College, Jersey, was in the Channel Islands when they were occupied by the Germans. Many months elapsed before his wife's family in Croydon learned that he was safe and well.

R.N.C. (DARTMOUTH) v R.A.F. (A.T.C.)
Lord's, August 12, 13, 1942

On Wednesday the bugle band of the Air Force Cadets attended.

SIR GEORGE ROBERT EDWARDS
(1908–2003)

He was at the heart of almost every development in British aviation for 40 years from biplanes to Concorde. He was also a skilful leg-break bowler, playing alongside the Bedser twins in club cricket, and married his two interests by insisting on the importance of backspin in the design of Barnes Wallis's bouncing bombs used in the Dambusters raids of 1943.

MISCELLANEA
[1943]

General Montgomery was an outstanding athlete at St. Paul's School, where he gained his colours for cricket and Rugby. The 1906 edition of *Wisden* referred to Montgomery's fighting qualities in these words: 'When the full team were able to play, they gave a good account of themselves, and showed their ability to play an uphill game, Cooper and Montgomery against Merton College putting on over 100 for the last wicket when a severe defeat seemed impending.'

When General Montgomery called on the Eighth Army for the supreme effort which led to the brilliant victory in Libya he used that great phrase, 'Hit him (Rommel) for six right out of Africa.'

* * *

F. R. Brown, the England and Surrey cricketer, revealed in a postcard to MCC that the following seventeen British sportsmen were in a prison camp in Italy:—Cricketers: F. R. Brown, W. E. Bowes (England and Yorkshire), C. G. Toppin (Worcestershire and Casuals F.C.), J. W. Bowley (MCC), H. Beaumont (Yorkshire II), R. H. Catterall (South Africa), T. W. T. Baines (Transvaal), Fellshaw (Natal), Henderson (N. Transvaal), Saby (N. Transvaal), Sir de Villiers Graaf (Oxford University); Rugby Football: A. D. S. Roncoroni (England, Richmond, East Midlands), C. W. Wilton (Cambridge U.), B. G. Gray (South Africa); Hockey: C. E. N. Wyatt (England), A. C. Glover; Squash: B. G. Barnes.

* * *

Sergt.-Pilot Walter Hamilton Arthur Mailey, son of Arthur Mailey, former Australian Test cricketer, was awarded the D.F.M. for leadership of 18 Kittyhawk fighters which shot down 20 enemy machines in an air battle in the Middle East.

* * *

Sir William Becher, pre-war captain of Sussex Second XI, besides being wounded in Libya, was twice captured by the enemy but escaped each time.

* * *

Mr. A. E. Newton, old Oxford Blue and Somerset wicket-keeper from 1880 to 1914, played for a team of veterans against schoolboys at Taunton in August 1943 when within a month of his 80th birthday. He stumped three batsmen and ran out another.

MISCELLANEA
[1944]

General Sir Miles Dempsey, Commander of the Second Army, an enthusiastic cricketer, captained Shrewsbury in 1914 and played for Sussex v Northamptonshire at Northampton in 1919.

* * *

General M. B. Burrows, who, as a member of the British Military Mission, accompanied Mr. Winston Churchill to Russia, scored 42 not out for Eton against Harrow in 1912. At Oxford he played in the 1914 Freshmen's match, and in 1924, when county captain, headed both batting and bowling averages of Oxfordshire. As a fast bowler, he was a valuable member of many Army representative sides.

* * *

Lieut. Col. Pieter G. Van der Bijl, Oxford cricket Blue in 1932 and South Africa opening batsman against England in the 1938–39 Test match series, was badly wounded in Italy in August. Both ankles and his spine were fractured, but doctors considered permanent disability unlikely. A schoolmaster before the war, he rose to command a battalion, and in February 1943 was awarded the M.C.

* * *

Len Hutton, of Yorkshire and England, gave a bat to an Army unit, and the commanding officer presented it to Cecil Pepper of New South Wales for rapidly making a century against an English team in Palestine. Using this bat in Queensland, Pepper scored an amazing hundred in 24 minutes, his hits including ten 6's.

* * *

Flying-Officer A. E. Barras, who played cricket for the RAAF in England last summer, after being shot down over Libya, returned to Australia. Playing his first game for five years for Fitzroy, his old club, Barras took six wickets for 36 and scored 41.

NOTES BY THE EDITOR, 1944

In very different surroundings – Stalag Luft prison camp in East Prussia – Australia won a 'Test' match by three runs, the last England wicket falling to a wonderful catch off the last ball of the final over. The fieldsman at point lost his balance but rising with the ball in his right hand claimed victory as his reward. That catch gave J. E. Connolly, who was cricket secretary of Sydney University before the war, a match record of 13 wickets for 60 runs. At another prison camp, Stammlager, Australia won a triangular tournament, defeating England in the deciding match after a victory for each over New Zealand.

THE BIRMINGHAM FESTIVAL IN 1944

Special praise again was due to Councillor R. I. Scorer, who conquered manifold difficulties in inaugurating the Festival week in 1942 when the ground was in a derelict condition, and his effervescing enthusiasm and initiative reaped a just reward in 1944. Besides securing the help of many Test and county players—and entertaining them handsomely—he paid every possible attention to the needs of the public. Each score-card contained on the reverse a diagram of fielding positions and, over a loud-speaker, Councillor Scorer maintained a constant service of comment and information on the play and players. Music during lunch and tea, news items, and even a 'Lost Property' and 'Missing People' bureau, increased the general enjoyment. The crowds certainly appreciated all this thought, and, as the microphone was used discreetly only between the intervals of actual cricket, the players agreed that it did not affect their concentration on the game.

A large number of schoolboys attended the five games and enjoyed the freedom of the playing area during the intervals—a thing unknown on the ground in peace-time. Although they took full advantage of the privilege, not once was trespass made on the square itself, marked only by small whitewash circles on the turf. A special enclosure for wounded soldiers and the hospitality extended to them also struck a note of comradeship.

LORD'S XI v PUBLIC SCHOOLS
Lord's, August 11, 12, 1944

During the first innings a flying bomb exploded less that 200 yards from Lord's. Pieces of soil fell on the pitch, but the players, particularly the boys, most of whom had never experienced such an attack, stopped only while the bomb was seen hurtling down. The break in the game lasted little more than half a minute, and the spectators, some of whom had thrown themselves flat under seats for protection, showed their appreciation of the boys' pluck with hearty hand-claps.

AUSTRALIAN SERVICES XI
[1945]

There were two repatriated prisoners-of-war in the party – R. G. Williams and D. K. Carmody. Despite spending nearly four years in a German prison camp after being shot down in a Maryland aircraft during the Libyan campaign, Williams soon found his form and he claimed Hutton as a victim four times in the five games with England. Carmody, released by the Russians after one year in Germany, failed to produce the form he showed before his capture. Within a week of getting back to England he joined the side; he might have done better as a batsman if he had rested longer.

ENGLAND v AUSTRALIA
Old Trafford, August 20, 21, 22, 1945

As at Sheffield, this match outside London was staged by the Inter-Services Sports Committee, and German prisoners were paid three farthings an hour for painting the buildings (outside) and putting certain parts of the bomb-scarred ground in a safe condition.

CRICKET IN IRAQ
[2003]

The Australian 'Digger' in desert army fatigues takes strike with his red plastic bat, his rifle and pistol a handy arm's length away (making intimidation of batsmen a risky enterprise). When a dust storm blows up, the 'pang' of the tennis ball hitting the empty ration drum which serves as stumps is his only way of knowing his fate, or even if a ball has been bowled, let alone picking what his British or American coalition comrades have bowled. That's if he's not running for cover to make way for an incoming chopper to land on the pitch, the American general's helipad. The threat of inconsistent bounce on the Hessian cover is negated by the batsmen's love of the big hit, necessary because the ball decelerates quickly on the dusty outfield. This is especially true of the Americans, who make up the numbers if we are short for Australia v England. They are also the subject of accusations of chucking. Normal standards are further watered down at the indoor matches held in the cavernous 30-room North Palace in Baghdad, untouched by looters and occupied by troops of the Royal Australian Navy. Under the gaze of busts of Saddam Hussein in heroic poses, games are played in the ballroom-sized anteroom. A ball landing on the first landing of the massive marble staircase is a four, on the second level a six. Our bowlers take aim at the stumps, a garish reproduction 17th-century French reclining lounger placed end on, making wicket-keepers redundant. Players are given stern pre-match warnings against hitting the throne in the foyer for reasons of cultural sensitivity. At the time of writing, the Baghdad Ashes are to be inaugurated, comprising a 50-calibre bullet case containing the ashes of a broken leg from an equally tasteless reproduction 15th-century chair, used as the wicket for our first game. When the security situation improves, it is hoped we will play on the old cricket pitch, a remnant from the British days.

Latest from Iraq The Baghdad Ashes were abandoned owing to dangerous conditions – not from any hazards of war, but simply because temperatures were too high and the surface not up to it. The venue was within the grounds of the Palace of Abu Guyarb, now a helipad and the largest area we could find guaranteed free from mines or unexploded ordnance. The wicket was made up of some wooden doors from a nearby bombed-out building, which provided interesting bounce. And in the absence of protective gear other than combat helmets, it was decided to play for fun rather than putting national honour at stake. Worst of all, there was a total alcohol ban in force.

CRICKET IN IRAQ
[2006]

The kids of Basra The children of southern Iraq do not currently have much to laugh about. Thanks to a donation of Kwik Cricket sets from the ECB, we set out to give some of them the chance to experience the sheer pleasure of playing cricket. The logistics of such an innocent exercise are not like those elsewhere. Movement outside the base locations is not that easy for Coalition Forces. The threat is high. To get access to the schools you must first arrange to join a patrol heading in the right direction. Eventually, I was driven to a small village school near Basra Air Station as part of a heavily armed RAF Regiment patrol; I travelled in one armoured Land Rover, the one behind had a

.50 calibre heavy machine gun. We were all wearing body armour and helmets and the members of the patrol constantly scanned every direction for danger. The temperature in our vehicles was close to 50°C. Once we got to the village school, the patrol formed a 'ring of steel'. Within the now-secure environment, I was introduced to the school's sports mistress, clad from head to foot in black, although her face was uncovered. The children I met were wide-eyed with curiosity, and a little uncertain as to the concept of bat-and-ball games. However, after some simple explanation of the basic rules of cricket (through an interpreter) and a quick demonstration by members of the RAF, the Iraqi children joyfully hit the ball around the playground. I duly handed over the set to the games mistress and she in turn professed to be keen to allow her charges to play on a regular basis. Next stop Lord's? Well, maybe not in the near future, but if this brings some enjoyment to children who are living in some very challenging conditions, then mission accomplished. Our patrol back to base was thankfully uneventful. ANDREW BANKS

The Baghdad Ashes The Baghdad Cricket Ground, part of the British Embassy compound, which provided a diversion in the early days of the occupation, was lost to the game when it was subdivided into three tennis courts, which could then be converted into a mini-football pitch. But after the 2005 Ashes, we Aussies – fed up with the jibes at the British Embassy bar ('the whinge bar') – were stung into action by that English fluke and began a desperate search for a block of barren ground, free of landmines and any other unexploded ordinance. This failed, and eventually we went back to the old pitch, making the best of the all-weather surface. It was agreed we would play the best of three. The opening match was memorable in more ways than one. Jack Straw, then British Foreign Secretary, was in town, and agreed to bowl the opening ball (a sort of left-arm grenade lob). Sky TV was in attendance and, as we later learned, the game was shown that night in the UK for well over a nanosecond. Two rubbish bins formed the stumps; we had a weighty rubber ball and genuine bats. Because of the security situation, full combat body armour and helmets had to be worn by fielders and batsmen alike; the participants looked more like deep-sea divers than cricketers. We did have a TV umpiring facility, thanks to the six perimeter security cameras round the compound which came in handy when we had to settle a run-out. Helped by a couple of grade cricketers from Melbourne, we bowled the Poms out for 47. We looked forward to two more matches, as agreed. Then disaster struck in the form of two rockets which landed, but failed to explode, in the sand adjacent to the pitch just prior to the scheduled commencement of play the following morning. It was enough for our English colleagues, without consultation, to call off the rest of the series.

Ashes in the Desert The Australian Army secured the country's first, but not last, Ashes success of 2006 by beating British Forces in the 'Ashes in the Desert', a 30-over charity game at Basra Air Station, by three wickets. The Australians received a replica urn, and a congratulatory e-mail from Ricky Ponting.

Extreme Fielding

REV. WALTER MONEY
(1848–1924)

In 1871 Oxford beat Cambridge by eight wickets. Of the many stories that have enshrouded the Cobden match—the Balaclava Charge of the cricket field—Money himself contributed one of the best, telling how Jack Dale, when reproached for allowing a simple catch at point to go unheeded, apologised by saying, 'I'm awfully sorry, Walter, I was looking at a lady getting out of a drag.'

A. N. HORNBY
(1847–1924)

A characteristic tale of the famous batsman concerned the Gentlemen and Players match at the Oval in 1881. Hornby and W. G. Grace had given the amateurs a capital start when, from a powerful drive, Hornby was magnificently caught high up in the long field by William Gunn, who stood some 6ft. 3in. in height. 'Bad luck, Monkey' said a friend as Hornby passed into the pavilion. 'Yes,' answered Hornby, 'no one but a damned giraffe would have got near it.'

REV. V. F. A. ROYLE
(1854–1929)

It was for his brilliant fielding that Royle will be chiefly remembered. He was ambidextrous, very quick on his feet and smart in return, preventing many a run which would have been successful against a less expert fieldsman. Tom Emmett's famous remark to a brother Yorkshireman, who called to him for a sharp run when Royle was at cover point, was a practical tribute to the fieldsman's excellence: 'Woa, mate, there's a policeman,' called Emmett, and there was no more attempt at a sharp run.

NOTTINGHAMSHIRE v NORTHAMPTONSHIRE
Nottingham, July 4, 5, 6, 1910

Seymour was out in a curious manner. Standing outside his crease, he placed a ball into the hands of the wicket-keeper and was run out.

REFLECTIONS BY PATSY HENDREN
[1937]

In connection with fielding, a funny thing once happened to me when on an MCC tour in Australia. Between fixtures, I was journeying into the Bush by motor-car with a colleague when we stopped to watch a cricket match. One of the players, unaware of our identity, approached and asked if, as his team was a man short, one of us would play. I had already been in the field for two and half days, but I yielded to persuasion and, rigged out in borrowed gear, was put in the deep field at the bottom of a pronounced slope, from where I could see nothing at all of the cricket. For hour after hour I fielded there, throwing the ball back at intervals until, at long last, I caught one. I ran to the top of the hill and announced with some satisfaction that I had made a catch. To my consternation, I was informed that the other team's innings had closed and that I had caught one of my own side!

HERBERT STRUDWICK
(1880–1970)

It is of interest to note that a lady set 'Struddy' on the path to becoming the world's most celebrated wicket-keeper. As a choir-boy at Mitcham, his birthplace, he took part in matches under the supervision of the daughter of the vicar, a Miss Wilson. Then about 10 years old, Strudwick habitually ran in from cover to the wicket to take returns from the field. Observing how efficiently he did this, Miss Wilson once said: 'You ought to be a wicket-keeper.' From that point, Strudwick became one.

FRED PRICE
(1902–1969)

In 1937 he set up a record, since equalled but not surpassed, when he took seven catches in the Yorkshire first innings at Lord's.

After the match, a lady approached Price with congratulations upon his feat. 'I was so thrilled with your performance, Mr. Price,' she said, 'that I nearly fell over the balcony.' With mock gravity, Price responded: 'If you had, madam, I would have caught you as well!'

OXFORD UNIVERSITY v AUSTRALIANS
Oxford, May 4, 5, 6, 1938

On the last day when Walker had a damaged finger, Fingleton, who like Hassett hit during this match his first century in England, stumped three men.

ENGLAND v INDIA
The Oval, August 17, 19, 20, 1946

Merchant started for a short run, was sent back by Mankad but moved too slowly and Compton, running behind the bowler from mid-on, kicked the ball on to the stumps – an incident reminiscent of that by Joe Hulme, another Arsenal and England forward, who in the same way dismissed Iddon of Lancashire in 1938 when Middlesex visited Old Trafford.

ESSEX v WARWICKSHIRE
Ilford, June 3, 5, 6, 1950

Kardar, at slip, smartly 'stumped' Vigar off Hollies, but as the wicket-keeper did not remove the bails the bowler under Laws 41 and 42 was not credited with the wicket.

ENGLAND v WEST INDIES
Lord's, June 16, 17, 18, 20, 21, 1966

Even the new ball did not disturb Parks and D'Oliveira and their partnership of 48 was in full sail when Parks drove back so fast that the ball went off D'Oliveira's heel and bounced back from the broken wicket. Hall, with commendable presence of mind, swept up the ball and pulled up the stump with both hands without the South African making any attempt to recover his ground.

ENGLAND V WEST INDIES
Scarborough, August 26, 1976

Barlow was one of the principals in a freak incident which baffled players and spectators and defeated the umpires. When 71 he answered Knott's call for a single when the wicket-keeper played the ball to fine leg. Holding's throw hit the nearest stumps with Barlow well in and he immediately called Knott for a second. However, the ricochet beat Barlow down the pitch and hit the stumps at the bowler's end with both batsmen in mid-pitch, a fact confirmed by the television cameras. There was a pause of a few seconds before Clive Lloyd, seeing the bails off at both ends, appealed to Umpire Jepson, who gave not out.

NEW ZEALAND v AUSTRALIA
Christchurch, February 18, 19, 20, 22, 23, 1977

When Lillee bowled the last over, to Congdon, he had every fieldsman in a line from the wicket keeper to a point position – a ploy repeated at Auckland, so that a picture could be provided for the cover of a new book by Chappell.

NINE CATCHES IN AN INNINGS

Les Andrews, keeping wicket in a first-grade match in Sydney, for Bankstown-Canterbury against Sydney University in November 1982, held nine catches during Sydney's innings of 236. So far as is known this constitutes a world record. The tenth wicket fell to a run out at the bowler's end.

ENGLAND v NEW ZEALAND
Lord's, July 24, 25, 26, 28, 29, 1986

It would hardly be a drawn Lord's Test without rain and bad light plus a much-discussed, if short-lived controversy. This came on the second day when French, England's injured wicket-keeper, was replaced by the former England wicket-keeper, R. W. Taylor. French had been struck on the back of the helmet when he turned away from a Hadlee bouncer, the resulting cut requiring three stitches and the blow leaving him groggy until after the weekend. Athey deputised for two overs at the start of New Zealand's innings until Taylor could hurry round the ground – from his duties as host for Cornhill, the match's sponsor – and equip himself with an assortment of borrowed kit, although he did, far-sightedly, have his own gloves in his car. Despite having retired from first-class cricket two years earlier, Taylor, at the age of 45, kept almost without blemish. He did his old job until the 76th over, near the lunch interval on Saturday, after which R. J. Parks of Hampshire, following his grandfather and father, appeared in a Test match. However, Parks, a more authentic substitute, should have been on stand-by at the start of play because recovery from such a head wound is seldom immediate. French finally assumed his appointed role for one ball on Monday morning. All these switches were made with the generous permission of New Zealand's captain, Coney. With substitutes also needed for Willey and Foster and for Coney and Jeff Crowe, 29 players took the field at various times.

WESTERN AUSTRALIA v NEW SOUTH WALES
Perth, December 20, 21, 22, 23, 1990

Both Mark (446 minutes, 343 balls, one six, 35 fours) and Steve Waugh (339 balls, 24 fours) reached their highest scores, and they so dominated the vaunted Western Australian pace attack that Zoehrer had to discard his wicket-keeping duties to bowl leg-breaks.

UCBSA PRESIDENT'S XI v INDIANS
Verwoerdburg, November 6, 7, 8, 9, 1992

Prabhakar swung the ball freely in the humidity, helping More to three of his six dismissals. One ball from Prabhakar, however, brought six byes: it struck a helmet on the ground behind More and the umpires unexpectedly ruled that the batsmen had completed a single before the five-run penalty came into force.

ZIMBABWE v SOUTH AFRICA
Harare, October 13, 14, 15, 16, 1995

The Zimbabweans were forced to wait before buying their opponents a post-match drink, as South Africa immediately embarked upon a lengthy fielding practice.

MATABELELAND v MASHONALAND
COUNTRY DISTRICTS
Bulawayo, April 19, 20, 21, 1996

Home captain Wayne James dominated the match in a manner unprecedented in world cricket. He made nine dismissals in the Districts' first innings, to equal the world record of Tahir Rashid, who caught eight and stumped one for Habib Bank v PACO in 1992-93. In the second innings, he added four more to set a new record of 13 dismissals in a match, beating 12 by Edward Pooley for Surrey v Sussex in 1868, Don Tallon for Queensland v New South Wales in 1938-39 and Brian Taber for New South Wales v South Australia in 1968-69. He also scored 99 in both Matabele innings, though he might have reached his century in the second if the wicket-keeper had not conceded four byes to give the home side victory. Only one player is known to have scored two 99s in a first-class match, Amay Khurasia of Madhya Pradesh, against Vidarbha in 1991-92. He was also left stranded in the second innings – but did not break the world wicket-keeping record.

Foreign and Unfamiliar Fields

CRICKET IN THE WINTER OF 1878–79

All England will remember, with a shiver and a shudder, the long, sad, and severe winter of 1878–79, commencing, as it did in October '78, and continuing – with more or less severity – up to the middle of May '79; and even then the cold, nipping, bronchitis creating winds seemed loth to leave the land they had so sorely stricken with distress, disease, and death. But there is no black cloud without its silver lining, and one bright spot in this dark winter was its severity and length enabled more

CRICKET MATCHES ON THE ICE

to be played than were ever before played in the course of one winter.

R. GILLOTT'S SIDE v B. CHATTERTON'S SIDE

Played by the Members of the Sheffield Club, December 17, 1878, on the ice that covered the Duke of Devonshire's Swiss Cottage Pond. One condition of the match was that any one obtaining 20 runs should retire. Mr W. Shearstone of Mr Gillott's team was the only man who made the 20, the next highest scorers being Mr R. Gillott with 13, and T. Rowbotham (Mr Chatterton's side) also with 13. They played seven a side, Mr Gillott's team having the best of the match by 11 runs. Totals: – Mr Gillott's Side, 46. Mr Chatterton's Side, 35.

CAMBRIDGE TOWN v CAMBRIDGE UNIVERSITY

Played on the Ice at Grantchester, December 17, 18, 19, 1878
Mr Coxall of Grantchester having flooded upwards of twenty acres of land in his meadows for the purpose of skating, a cricket match was arranged to be played by the above-named teams under the captaincies of Mr C. Pigg, of Peterhouse, and the ex-All England cricketer, 'Bob' Carpenter. The townsmen were first at the wickets, and after two hours' play on the first day they had lost nine wickets for 193 runs,

Newman leading the score with a well played 68, which included a 6, three 5s, three 4s and six 3s. The next day 'Bob' Carpenter (not out 4) was accompanied to the wicket by 'Dan' Hayward, and this pair were not separated until they had been seventy minutes at wickets, and augmented the score by 132 runs, when Hayward was clean bowled for 44; and – in that same over – Carpenter sent the ball into the hands of cover point, having then 89 runs to his credit, mainly made by two 5s (leg hit and cut), one 4, and a dozen 3s. The innings terminated for 326 runs. The ice was very bad when the 'Varsity's innings was commenced by Lilley, and Von-Scott; the former was bowled when only 8 runs had been made. W. Deedes then joined Scott and they succeeded in keeping their wickets intact for nearly another half-hour when the stumps were drawn, the score standing at 61 for one wicket. The match was resumed on the Thursday, several large scores were made, and when time was called the 'Varsity had scored 274 runs for the loss of four wickets. The match was drawn.

LORD HENRY NEVILL'S SIDE v MR WILLIAMS' SIDE
Played on the Ice at Eridge Castle, Kent, February 1, 1879

The Marquis of Abergavenny, with that considerate courtesy characteristic of his race, had the gates of his park thrown open to all who chose to enter and witness the grand Fete on the frozen water of the great lake at his Lordship's seat – Eridge Castle. The Marquis and a distinguished company were present, and some 2000 other visitors assembled, who appeared to heartily enjoy the jolly games of Hockey, played at one end of the lake, and cricket at the other. As to the cricket match both Captains were (as Captains should be) well in front of their men, Lord Henry Neville taking the lead with 70, not out – pronounced by the critics. 'A remarkably good innings, his lordship having been frequently applauded for the dexterity he displayed, and the command he evinced over skates and bat'. But Mr Williams ran a close second to his lordship, both as to skill on skates and run getting, for he scored an innings of 68 in good form; and, if it could have been

played out to the pleasant end, the game would doubtless have had a most interesting finish, for when the early darkness stopped play Mr Williams' side had two wickets to fall, with only 53 runs to make to win.

This was the last match played on the ice in that terribly severe and distressful winter, for on the following day (Sunday, February 2) a rapid thaw set in, continuing throughout the Monday; and although winter and rough weather subsequently returned, and discomfortingly continued with us up to the middle of May, there was no further frost sufficiently severe to form and fix ice capable of playing cricket on; and so, with Lord Henry Nevill's match at Eridge Park, was ended the never-to-be-forgotten Cricket on the Ice Season of 1878–79.

SHAW'S TEAM IN AUSTRALIA, 1884–85

The team left Plymouth in the S.S. 'Orient' on Friday, September 18, 1884, and reached Suez at eleven o'clock on the morning of Thursday, October 2. In accordance with a previous arrangement a match was played against Twenty-two of the Army, Navy, and Residents of Suez. The scene of the contest was a plain of sand, in the centre of which a piece of cocoanut matting was tightly stretched.

THE ROAR OF THE GREASEPAINT
[1993]

David Rayvern Allen writes: The only time that county cricketers as a team have played the game on the West End stage was when the impresario Sir Oswald Stoll mounted a variety spectacle for his winter season of 1908 at the Coliseum. The billing read Surrey v Middlesex, with four professionals from The Oval captained by Alan Marshal, against the same number from Lord's led by Albert Trott. J. T. Hearne and 19-year-old 'Patsy' Hendren were in the Middlesex side. The audience were given a scorecard to keep tabs on the official scorer who was on the stage itself. The painting on the backcloth was of a village green surrounded by trees, depicting a pastorally idyllic summer's day. The pitch was restricted to 15 yards and adapted rules applied; for instance, a hit meant a run had to be attempted. The runs scored at each performance were cumulative and each morning the revised score was posted outside the theatre. At one performance, the net which protected orchestra and audience from the four-ounce ball could not be raised for some reason and the game proceeded with those in the stalls acting as extra fielders. Fortunately, no one was hurt. At the end of a week, Middlesex just managed to beat Surrey.

SIR PELHAM WARNER
(1873–1963)

He often used to relate that his first recollections of cricket were of batting on a marble gallery at his home, The Hall, Port of Spain, Trinidad, to the bowling of a black boy who rejoiced in the name of Killebree (Humming Bird). At thirteen and a half he came to England, but before that he had three years at Harrison College, Barbados, and at thirteen had gained a place in the first XI.

The whole course of his life was altered by Lord Hawke's invitation to tour the West Indies, and on January 13, 1897, he began the first of many journeys across the seas. As it happened the opening match was against Trinidad and he had the distinction of scoring 119, the first hundred that had ever been scored in the Island in an important match. Scores of black men rushed across the ground at the end of his innings shouting out 'I taught you, Mr. Pelham. You play well, Sir; we are proud of you.'

WHEN THREE-DAY CRICKET WAS WORTHWHILE
[1974]

C. T. Bennett writes: When I went with the Hon. F. S. G. Calthorpe's MCC team to the West Indies in 1925–26, the spirit of both players and spectators was remarkable and the crowds levelled far more criticism at their own cricketers than they did at us. Instead of having, as is sometimes the case nowadays, to avoid flying bottles, the deep fieldsmen were frequently offered a swig from a bottle of rum by an onlooker! I recall with glee one match in which the Hon. Lionel (later Lord) Tennyson was fielding at third man when a coloured woman of extremely ample proportions dashed on to the field and said to him: 'How would you like to be a fat old bitch like me?' Lionel's response was to give her a resounding kiss, to the cheers of the crowd.

NOTES BY THE EDITOR, 1951

At the John Wisden & Co., Ltd., centenary luncheon in May, to Mr Harold Wilson fell the task of proposing the toast of 'This Wonderful Century'. He confessed that he was no cricketer himself, but he remarked: 'I am a Yorkshireman, and cricket is never far from a Yorkshireman's thoughts.' Then he amused us with an account of the last time he played cricket. He said it was in Moscow when he was there for trade talks with the Russians. 'There was one Sunday afternoon, during a lull in the negotiations, when my delegation repaired to some woods not far from Moscow. A few weeks afterwards, following the breakdown of the discussions, the Moscow Press, who seem to have observed our innocent pastime, came out with an account of the "orgies and strange pirouettes by the lakeside of the English delegation".' Continuing his reminiscence, Mr Wilson told this story:

'My second over was interrupted by a gentleman from the NKVD or Ogpu, who was appointed to follow us around and see that we came to no harm. He stood in the middle of the pitch and remonstrated with us in a very long Russian speech which I understood came to this – that we could not do that there! He was supported by two men who came up on horseback with rifles. I persuaded him, after some negotiation, to take up his position at square leg, out of the way of even my bowling. The episode closed with the NKVD man's failure to make any attempt to catch a ball – and after that my opinion of the Russian secret police fell even lower.' Mr Wilson suggested that the incident should be recorded in *Wisden* as the 'only case of a catch being missed at square leg by a member of the NKVD off an off-spinner by a visiting British minister'.

CRICKET IN ETHIOPIA
[1965]

Perhaps the day may not be far distant when Ethiopia will be challenging England and Australia to Test Matches. Until a few months ago cricket was unknown in that vast country. An Australian doctor resident there, Dr. R. H. J. Hamlin, put forward the idea that it would be a good thing for morale if someone from Australia could go there and introduce the game. So W. A. Oldfield, who holds the wicket-keeping record for Tests between England and Australia with 90 victims in 38 matches, spent a month converting the natives to cricket. In that time he taught the game at four schools. He brought with him several complete sets of cricket-gear, including bats, balls, pads, gloves and coir matting. The matting was laid over couch grass and the native boys took so readily to a game completely strange to them that before Oldfield left they played a charity match in which at the age of 66 he took part. The highlight of Bert Oldfield's visit was a twenty-minute audience with the Emperor, Haile Selassie, who accepted a bat for competition between the schools, two of which have English head-masters, presented by Sir Robert Menzies as a gesture of goodwill from Australia to Ethiopia.

THE CHINESE YEAR OF THE CRICKET

Following a short three-match tour to the People's Republic of China, undertaken in August, 1983, by the St George's Cricket Club of Hong Kong, it is hoped that the All China Sports Federation may set up a team of indigenous cricketers. A fair crowd, including a sprinkling of bemused Chinese, watched the matches between the St George's Club and teams composed mainly of diplomats, expatriate businessmen, journalists and students from the United Kingdom, Australia, India,

Pakistan, New Zealand and Africa. The Beijing Cricket Club, c/o The British Embassy, The People's Republic of China, would be pleased to hear from would-be visiting sides.

ALL TEN WICKETS FOR MALAYSIA

Playing for Malaysia in the Saudara Cup match against Singapore, at Kuala Lumpur in December 1983, K. Saker, bowling at medium pace, took ten wickets for 25 runs in Singapore's first innings. Malaysia won the match by ten wickets. The Saudara Cup series was inaugurated in 1970. Of the fourteen matches played, each side has won three and eight have been drawn.

CRICKET IN ANTARCTICA

What was almost certainly the most southerly game of cricket ever played, and the coldest, took place in Antarctica, 700 kilometres from the South Pole, on January 11, 1985, between two teams drawn from the 60 scientists, lawyers, environmentalists and administrators engaged in an international workshop being held at the Beardmore South Camp and concerned with the Antarctica Treaty. New Zealand's representative on the Treaty, Christopher Beeby, captained the Gondwanaland Occasionals with players from Australia, New Zealand and South Africa. A British delegate to the Conference, Arthur Watts, captained the Beardmore Casuals, a basically British team. The stumps were improvised, the pitch, such as it was, had been rolled by a Hercules transport aircraft, and the 'midnight sun' allowed play to continue until 11.00 p.m. The Occasionals (129) beat the Casuals (102) by 27 runs.

CRICKET IN THE NETHERLANDS
[1990]

In September the beach cricket open championship was a great success on the Wadden Sea island of Schiermonnikoog.

NEPAL
[1992]

In Nepal cricket is second only to soccer in popularity. The Rameshwore Memorial Shield was won by Kathmandu Khel Mandal. Their player Sri Nivas Rana was named as Man of the Series and he was awarded a television set, courtesy of Khetri Sausages.

CRICKET GROUNDS IN 1992

The annual Glamorgan match sponsored by Taff Ely Council has been switched from Ynysangharad Park, Pontypridd, where there were problems caused by restrictions on car parking as well as pronunciation.

THE ABN-AMRO ICC TROPHY
Sharjah, 1993–94

From the moment their players arrived in Nairobi there were rumours about Mercedes-per-man win bonuses and dark mutterings from other teams that the oil-rich Gulf state had imported a team with the sole purpose of winning a World Cup place. Members of the organising committee subjected the Emirates' hierarchy to a four-hour grilling on the residential status of each player, but manager Vikram Kaul maintained throughout that his side were only abiding by rules that they had no part in framing and the 15 members of his squad who were born on the Indian sub-continent (all except the captain, Sultan Zarawani) were all now full-time employees in the Gulf and played cricket in their spare time. This was never disproved, but the bitterness spilled over into the celebration dinner. The UAE party walked out in protest against criticism levelled at them. As they left, the Kenyan Cricket Association chairman Basheer Mauladad told the gathering: 'We too can import slaves to win a tournament.'

CRICKET IN SOUTH KOREA
[1994]

Cricket revived in Korea in the late 1980s through the expatriate Indian community. It is played by six teams of nine a side (representing Australia, India, New Zealand, British Embassy, International All Stars and the Rest of the World) over 15 overs on a small, irregular-shaped soccer field controlled by the US Military in the UN Compound. We bowl only from one end, on a wicket that consists of bare ground, covered by one layer of rubberised matting overlaid by felt carpet; despite the small ground, bowlers tend to have the upper hand – shooters and fliers are par for the course. The scoring rules are modified but complex, taking into account the back wall (four if hit on the full), the willow tree (six) and the embankment with the blackberries.

CRICKET IN UNITED ARAB EMIRATES
[1995]

One match was abandoned owing to rain and the 'shoot-out' provision implemented. As per the tournament rules, six bowlers from one side had bowled one ball each at the unprotected stumps and five bowlers from the other side had also bowled one ball each. No one could hit the wicket; the players then objected to the rule. The organising secretary, Ali Anwar, a former first-class player in Pakistan, promptly took the ball. Still wearing his coat and tie, he hit the stumps with a leg-break straight away. The final bowler, the sixth one of the other side, then tried. He missed.

CRICKET IN SOUTH KOREA
[1995]

Domestic highlights included the six that was deflected off the non-striking batsman, Adrian Stephens of the British Embassy, and the moment when Ron Burnes of the All Star team attempted to field the ball at mid-on and disappeared down the drain that is a feature of the ground in Seoul. He re-emerged covered in mud and became known as 'the cricketer from the trench'.

CRICKET IN ASCENSION ISLAND
[1995]

Plans are afoot to return cricket to one of the world's most distinctive grounds. The barren, volcanic rock of Ascension Island in the South Atlantic is believed to be the only place where 'wedding stopped play' – to be resumed 40 minutes later as the last of the congregation left for the reception. The little Church of St Mary the Virgin is inside the boundary and, when it was restored in 1993, with a new slate roof, cricket moved to a new and larger ground at the island's RAF camp, where floodlit play is possible. However, the move has not been popular with the crowds (all things are relative – the total population is only 1,200) and Dr Sukhtanker, the resident surgeon and cricketing supremo, intends to take the game back to its traditional venue. Cricket on Ascension, uninhabited until the Royal Navy landed in 1815, took off when West Indian workers arrived in the mid-1960s to build a relay station. They started league cricket, which has been kept going by South Africans working for the cable company, and the RAF, who returned during the Falklands War. They have provided teaching input for the workers from St Helena who are employed here. Saint Helenians have a natural aptitude for the game, and have developed good technique, with two exceptions: the concrete strip offers little chance of spin, and the short boundaries – combined with American influence – have encouraged some towards the high baseball slog. The cricket field by the church, which used to be the army parade ground, is actually rolled volcanic ash, with not a blade of grass in sight, and the outfield is very fast. The ball used is a composite – a leather ball would be torn to shreds – and we need several per game there, to replace those which get stuck on the church roof or among the stores waiting to be loaded on the next ship. A dusty trade wind always blows across the pitch, but it is what people seem to prefer and it is indeed a fine setting, if you can find some shade: the four sides comprising the small, white church, a smooth, dark red, volcanic cone, the aging, arcaded barracks, and the dark blue ocean with its giant waves crashing in towards the anchorage below.

CRICKET IN FIJI
[1995]

Cricket in Fiji has various problems. In Lau, one of the traditional strongholds of the game, it has been affected by an increase in population and consequent encroachment on the village greens. Our national coach, Seci Sekinni, recently came across a ground where the pitch had been moved to accommodate new buildings, and as a result the outfielders were required to stand in the sea. It was thought this might be the origin of deep mid-off.

CRICKET IN KIRIBATI
[1996]

The most dramatic event of recent years came when the Kiribati XI flew to play an away fixture against the Republic of Tuvalu, formerly the Ellice Islands. Batting second, Kiribati were down to the last pair and needed six to win off the last ball. Darkness was falling fast and pressure mounting in more ways than one – the plane for the return journey had to take off from a narrow strip of land, between the ocean and the lagoon, with no landing lights. The batsman on strike was a strapping player called Tapatulu, a man of fearsome strength renowned locally for having once been lost at sea in a canoe for three months. It was a good-length ball, Tapatulu took a step outside leg stump and, with the well-used 'Len Hutton' team bat, despatched the ball over cow-shot corner for six.

CRICKET IN JAPAN
[1996]

Enthusiasm for cricket is high in Japan and the Gunma Cup, a two-day competition for Japanese men, enjoyed great popularity in its third year. Tokyo Bay CC won the cup for the second time. During the competition one of their players, Hiroki Minami, fell foul of a local rule which deducts five runs for a shot on to the nearby tennis court and was dismissed with a score of minus three.

CRICKET IN JAPAN
[1997]

The Japanese players remain hazy about the world game. A trivia quiz organised around the British Ambassador's Challenge Cup (for beginners) included the question: 'Name four past or present England Test players.' Three of the five teams named Atherton, two of them Hick; the only other names to appear were Lewis, Bradman, Donald and either Trevor Bailey or Bayley – they are the same in Japanese script. However, Japan's best fielder, Jin Shibata, is now known to his team-mates as 'Jonty'. As the game takes hold, an independent Japanese lexicon is appearing. Howzat is still used for an appeal, but backing up has become 'leading', a helmet is 'metto' and that most valuable piece of protective equipment is known as 'a cup'.

CRICKET IN THE FALKLAND ISLANDS
[1998]

The Oval can hold the entire population of the Falkland Islands: 4,000. The matting wicket traditionally favours bowlers, but only when they have the wind behind them. Those bowling into the wind regularly struggle to reach the opposite end.

NATIONAL VILLAGE CHAMPIONSHIP
[1998]

Apperley, from Gloucestershire, made less certain progress and had to call on overseas aid: Hugh Leeke, a key all-rounder who had been working on a carpentry job at Kazakhstan's national airport, flew home 36 hours before the semi-final against Horndon on the Hill of Essex. He took three for 48 and then opened the batting to help Apperley win by six wickets. His busy schedule saw him fly back to Kazakhstan at 4 a.m. the following morning, only to return for the final two weeks later.

NATIONAL CLUB CHAMPIONSHIP
[2000]

The victorious team Sheffield Collegiate included spinner John Hespe, a management consultant who had flown back (business class) from Philadelphia, where he was working on a deal, every weekend for two months to make sure Sheffield Collegiate reached the final for the first time.

CRICKET IN ICELAND
[2000]

The most northerly and most remarkable of cricketing nations arrived on the scene in 2000, not, in the normal fashion, through the efforts of exiles, but owing to the extraordinary vision of a handful of Icelanders. The story of Icelandic cricket began at the University of Iceland a few years ago when some students caught a glimpse of the game on Sky News. 'Everyone was dressed in white,' said one of them, Ragnar Kristinsson, 'with pressed trousers, and we wanted to do the same.' But none of the TV channels available in Iceland showed more than snatches of this mysterious game. However, in 1999 Kristinsson was on holiday in Cyprus during the great World Cup semi-final between Australia and South Africa, and was entranced again. The following Sunday he and a friend were in London, and decided they had to be near Lord's for the final. Outside, they met some Pakistanis, leaving in disgust as their team hurtled to defeat, who readily handed over their tickets. Kristinsson was now firmly hooked. He wrote to the European Cricket Council, who sent a starter set of equipment, and a couple of teams emerged: Kylfan (Icelandic for 'the bat') in Reykjavik and Ungmennafelagid Glaumur in Stykkisholmer (believed to be the world's most northerly club, as well as the most unpronounceable). The teams mostly comprised native Icelanders, with coaching from some better-informed expats. Iceland's entry into international cricket came in September 2000 when Manchester barrister and aspirant Liberal Democrat politician, Jonathan Rule, decided this was the perfect venue for his stag night. He assembled a group of friends in a beautiful valley outside Reykjavik to take on the locals. With the help of the *émigrés*, the Icelanders scored 107 on a bumpy football pitch. The visitors (said to be swaying slightly at the crease after the previous evening's entertainment) lurched to 94 in fading light, watched by rather more journalists and cameras than their cricket usually justifies. The headline 'Iceland beats England at cricket' appeared in the following morning's paper.

CRICKET IN VANUATU
[2000]

I also heard a story from Justice Robert Kent QC, the Acting Chief Justice of Vanuatu, who told me about a match being played on the island of Santo. An old chief happened to wander past and took an interest. He said: '*Mi wantem pleiplei smol tisfala gem*' ('I would like to play'). There was no objection. When his turn came, he swung a bat for the first time in his life and hit a six. We think that this could be a record.

SAND MEN

As part of a 'Play the Aussie Team' competition sponsored by a brewery, Steve Waugh's Beach Boys (91) defeated Gold Coast pensioner Peter Dawson's Lite Ice All Stars (58) in an eight-over-a-side beach cricket game at Coogee in Sydney on January 17, 2000. Eight current Australian players were involved, being divided between the two teams, with a matting pitch, rubber ball, and plastic stumps and bats in use.

CRICKET IN CHILE
[2004]

La Dehesa remained unbeaten to win the Metropolitan Cup, defeating Las Condes in the final. La Dehesa player and national parachuting champion Anthony Adams jun. attracted everyone's attention when he arrived for a club game from the air, landing at fine leg, peeling off his gear and taking his place in the field at the very spot where he landed.

CRICKET IN BHUTAN
[2006]

Children from privileged families are sent to study in India. There they learn the game and bring it home, where cricket acquires a uniquely Bhutanese flavour. Players bow their heads in supplication to the cricketing gods before taking the field. 'We do not pray for victory,' says national captain Dhamber Singh Gurung. 'We pray for each other to give our best and to emerge complete from the competition.' The Dechephu Lhakhang temple in Thimphu is the spiritual home of Bhutan cricket, and cricketers visit before every tournament to invoke the protecting deities. The team has had some success, beating Myanmar in the 2006 ACC Trophy. But Bhutan is no place for bowlers: at that altitude, the ball simply flies off the bat. One bowler, Phuntsho Wangchuk, exasperated by being hammered, has resorted to storing his cricket balls in his father's humidor in order to make them 'heavier'. However, he may yet have to give up bowling for cheroot-smoking.

Distinguished Personages

A CENTURY IN THE FIJI ISLANDS, 1974

Philip Snow writes: England has seldom seen Royal cricketers. A midshipman on HMS *Bacchante*'s 1881 circumnavigation, Prince George (later King George V), played against Levuka, then the capital of Fiji. His score significantly is not remembered. Next day he was demoted to *Bacchante*'s 2nd XI against HMS *Cleopatra*; the Press reported that 'his score did not greatly affect the total'. When the Prince of Wales visited Levuka in 1970 for Fiji's Independence, he was shown the ground so little productive of regal runs; the Press described him as not unamused.

THE CENTENARY OF THE MARYLEBONE CLUB
Banquet at Lord's

On Wednesday, June 15th, 1887, the Centenary banquet of the Marylebone Club was held in the Tennis Court at Lord's Cricket Ground. The Hon. E. Chandos Leigh (president) occupied the chair and the company present included the French Ambassador (M. Waddington), the Right Hon. G. J. Goschen, MP, the Duke of Abercorn, Lord Latham, Lord G. Hamilton, MP, Lord Bessborough, Lord Clarendon, Lord Willoughby de Broke, Lord Londesborough, Lord Oxenbridge, Lord Darnley, Lord Winterton, Lord Downe, Lord Wenlock, Lord Lyttelton, Lord Belper, Lord Harris, Sir W. Hart-Dyke, MP, Sir A. L. Smith, Sir G. Berry, Sir Saul Samuel, Sir J. F. Garrick, Sir J. Chitty, Hon. W. Monk Jervis, Hon. Sir S. Ponsonby-Fane, Hon. E. Stanhope, MP, Hon. Alfred Lyttelton, Rev. T. A. Anson, Rev. G. J. Boudier, Rev. J. Hornby, Mr R. Broughton, Mr J. L. Baldwin, Mr W. Nicholson, Mr R. A. H. Mitchell, Mr C. E. Green, Mr A. Rutter, Rev. V. Royle, Mr W. N. Roe, Mr T. C. O'Brien, Mr J. G. Walker, Mr E. F. S. Tylecote, Mr J. Shuter, Mr W. W. Read, Mr W. G. Grace, Mr H. Perkins, Mr A. N. Hornby, Mr A. J. Webbe, Mr I. D.

Walker, Mr W. H. Patterson, Mr A. W. Ridley, Mr A. Appleby, Mr D. Buchanan, Mr V. E. Walker, Mr W. H. Hadow, Mr Courtney Boyle, etc. After the loyal toasts had been duly honoured, Mr. Justice Chitty proposed 'The Houses of Lords and Commons', coupled with the names of the Duke of Abercorn and the Right Hon. G. J. Goschen, the Chancellor of the Exchequer.

In the course of an excellent speech the Right Hon. Mr Goschen went on to say that, however important the matters might be which engaged his attention as a politician, there was one part of the daily paper to which he invariably directed his attention the first thing in the morning, and that was the part containing the scores of the cricket matches in course of progress.

The Earl of Bessborough then proposed 'Success to Cricket and the MCC', tracing in the course of his speech the career of the Club from its earliest beginnings.

The Chairman responded and Lord Lathom proposed 'The Distinguished Visitors', to which toast M. Waddington and Sir Saul Samuel replied.

Viscount Lewisham, MP, then proposed 'The Great Army of Cricketers', to which there were six responses: 'The Church' (the Rev. Dr Hornby, Provost of Eton), 'The Army' (the Right Hon. E. Stanhope, MP), 'The Navy' (the Right Hon. Lord George Hamilton, MP), 'The Bench and the Bar' (the Hon. Mr Justice A. L. Smith), 'Medicine' (Mr W. G. Grace), and 'the Cricket Counties' (Lord Harris).

After his response to this toast, Lord Harris proposed the last toast of the evening, 'The Press', and in so doing bore full and generous testimony to the careful accuracy with which cricket matches were recorded in the papers, and to the large share with the Press had in promoting the popularity of the national game. Then, with the toast, 'Our Next Merry Meeting', a memorable evening came to an end.

LONDON COUNTY v SURREY
Crystal Palace, May 3, 4, 5, 1900

On the third day Sir George White, recently back in England after the siege of Ladysmith, drove on to the ground with Lady White and had an enthusiastic reception.

NAVY & ARMY v AUSTRALIAN &
SOUTH AFRICAN FORCES
Lord's, August 18, 1917

Arranged for the benefit of Lady Lansdowne's Officers' Families' Fund, this match, owing to a showery morning, did not attract as large a company as that between the English Army and Australian Army on the same ground, five weeks earlier. General Plumer and General Horne wired to P. F. Warner their good wishes for the success of the match, and among those present was Admiral Jellicoe.

WILLIAM L. KELLY
(1876–1968)

An amusing story is told of his visit to England. During a match at The Oval, he was said to have placed a notice on the door of the Australian dressing-room which read: 'Nobody admitted without manager's authority.' The Oval, of course, forms part of the Duchy of Cornwall, which provided a source of revenue to the then Prince of Wales, now the Duke of Windsor. The Prince attended the match, saw the notice and told Kelly: 'You can't keep me out. I'm your landlord!'

NEW SOUTH WALES v SOUTH AUSTRALIA
Sydney, January 17, 18, 20, 1936

Abandoned. Rain prevented play on the first day, and owing to the death of King George V, there was no cricket on the last day.

H. M. KING GEORGE VI
(1895–1952)

When Prince Albert he performed the hat-trick on the private ground on the slopes below Windsor Castle, where the sons and grandsons of Edward VII used to play regularly. A left-handed batsman and bowler, the King bowled King Edward VII, King George V and the present Duke of Windsor in three consecutive balls, thus proving himself the best Royal cricketer since Frederick, Prince of Wales, in 1751, took a keen interest in the game. The ball is now mounted in the mess-room of the Royal Naval College, Dartmouth. King George VI, like his father, often went to Lord's when Commonwealth teams were playing there, and invariably the players and umpires were presented to His Majesty in front of the pavilion. He entertained the 1948 Australian team at Balmoral, and in his 1949 New Year's Honours Donald Bradman, the captain, received a Knighthood.

WILLIAM HENRY FERGUSON
(1880–1957)

'Fergie' was the best-known cricket scorer in the world.

When in England with the Australian team of 1948, 'Fergie' was presented to King George VI. That summer Bradman scored 2,428 runs. Said the King: 'Mr Ferguson, do you use an adding-machine when the Don is in?'

ENGLAND v AUSTRALIA
Fourth Victory Match
Lord's, August 6, 7, 8, 1945

Mr Clement Attlee, the Prime Minister, was present on the second day when Miller completed his effort, England being kept in the field until lunch-time.

SURREY v OLD ENGLAND
The Oval, May 23, 1946

The King and some 15,000 enthusiasts attended the one-day match arranged to celebrate the Centenary of the Surrey County Club and of Kennington Oval as a cricket ground.

The King, Patron of Surrey, accompanied by officials of the club, went on the ground, where all concerned in the game were introduced to him with the happiest of greetings. The band of the East Surrey Regiment was in attendance, and after the game a dance in the pavilion long room completed the festive occasion.

SURREY v OLD ENGLAND
The Oval, June 12, 1947

Field-Marshal Lord Montgomery, born at St Mark's vicarage overlooking the ground, the guest of honour, shook hands with both teams on the field.

A CENTURY IN THE FIJI ISLANDS, 1974

Philip Snow writes: The immediate result of the Fiji Association's foundation was organisation of a tour of New Zealand in 1948, the first truly representative Fijian one.

Ratu Sir George Thakombau, great grandson of King Thakombau, son of Ratu Pope Thakombau and now Fiji's first Governor-General since Independence, who was my Vice-captain, had a bare toe broken by a yorker half-way through the tour: it was fortunate that Ratu Sir Edward Thakombau was able to join us then on return from Oxford. Ratu Sir Kamisese Mara was in mid-course at Oxford where injury deprived him of a Blue. His father once hit me for the highest six I have ever seen – vanishing into the sky to descend vertically into a 70-foot coconut palm's crown.

KENT v HAMPSHIRE
Canterbury, July 30, August 1, 1949

On Monday, when over 14,000 people were present, the teams were introduced to the Duke of Edinburgh, who was accompanied on the field by Lord Harris, Kent Club President, and Lord Cornwallis, Lord Lieutenant of Kent.

EISENHOWER AT THE TEST

An historic day for cricket was December 8, 1959, when Mr Dwight Eisenhower, President of the United States of America, graced the Third Test of the series between Pakistan and Australia at the National Stadium, Karachi. It was the first occasion that the head of the United States has witnessed a Test match and he was seen in a very happy mood applauding attractive strokes by the batsmen and good work by the fielders.

NOTES BY THE EDITOR, 1965
PRIME MINISTERS AT CRICKET

Sir Robert Menzies, Prime Minister of Australia, is a familiar figure at Test matches in his own country and he generally makes a special effort to be present at Lord's when Australia meet England. Last year, with the Prime Ministers' Conference taking place in London in mid-July, Sir Robert watched the Third Test at Headingley and had the good fortune to see Australia gain a splendid victory in the only match of the series brought to a definite conclusion. Sir Alec Douglas-Home, who made his name as a cricketer at Eton and for Middlesex when he was Lord Dunglass, paid a brief visit to the Old Trafford Test, as did his successor, Mr. Harold Wilson. Another Prime Minister, Mr. Ian Smith, of Rhodesia, went to Lord's in September when the Mashonaland Country Districts played Cross Arrows.

KENT v YORKSHIRE
Canterbury, July 31, August 1, 2, 1968

On Thursday, the Duke of Kent, Patron of Kent, paid his first visit to the St. Lawrence ground, accompanied by his wife, the Duchess, Patron of Yorkshire. On this notable day, Sir Robert Menzies, the former Australian Prime Minister, consented to become President of Kent in 1969.

PRESIDENT'S XI v WEST INDIES
Rawalpindi, October 19, 20, 21, 1986

Positive batting, following early losses, saw Qasim Omar and Ijaz Ahmed add 121 in even time before the close, and when both were caught off Harper on the third morning, Asif Mujtaba brought his own magic to bear on the afternoon for President Zia-ul-Haq, who was visiting the ground.

COLTS v PANADURA
Panadura, April 20, 21, 22, 2001

The last two sessions of the opening day were lost because of a VIP's helicopter landing on the ground.

SURREY v LANCASHIRE
Whitgift School, August 11, 12, 13, 2004

The Mayor of Croydon, Brenda Kirby, unwittingly delayed play by walking in front of the sightscreen as Bicknell prepared to bowl his first delivery for six weeks.

Umpires and the Laws

RUGBY v MARLBOROUGH
Lord's, July 28, 29, 1886

This proved to be one of the most interesting and well-contested of the public school matches played during the season of 1886, and it was made specially remarkable by a very singular incident which occurred late on the second afternoon. When Kitcat, the Marlborough captain, was disposed of it was discovered that Bengough, the Rugby captain, had by some oversight been allowed to go on twice at each end and in his first over from the pavilion wicket (the second time he had been on at that end) he got Kitcat caught at cover point. A long discussion ensued; but it was decided by the umpires that Kitcat, having been fairly caught, could not go in again. As a result, however, on the objection of the Marlborough captain, Bengough was not allowed to bowl another ball in the innings after he had completed his over. The affair gave rise to a great deal of correspondence, and indeed it was not thoroughly settled at the time whether or not the umpires had acted rightly. Of course it was a clear oversight on the part of the umpires that Bengough went on at this wrong end, but the universal opinion afterwards was that Kitcat having been fairly caught, the umpires had no option but to give him out.

ARTHUR HENRY DELME-RADCLIFFE
(1870–1950)

While batting for Hampshire against Somerset at Southampton in August, 1889, he was concerned in a curious incident. Thinking he was out stumped, Delme-Radcliffe began to walk towards the pavilion, but the appeal had not been upheld. Then a fieldsman pulled up a stump and he was given out 'run out', but in the meantime the other umpire had called 'over', so the batsman continued his innings.

OXFORD v CAMBRIDGE
Lord's, July 3, 4, 1893

There was one incident that caused a great deal of discussion in all cricket circles, and brought the question of an altercation of rule affecting the follow-on into the region of practical politics. Nine [Oxford] wickets were down for 95, and then on Wilson, the last man, joining Brain, an incident occurred which is likely to be talked about for a good many years to come. Three runs were added, making the score 98, 84 short of Cambridge's total, and Oxford thus required only 5 runs to save the follow-on. The two batsmen were then seen to consult together between the wickets, and it was at once evident to those who had grasped the situation that the Dark Blues were going to throw away a wicket in order that their side might go in again. Had one of them acted on his own account, it is probable that the object would have been gained, but Wells, who was bowling from the Pavilion end, saw at once what was intended and promptly set to work to frustrate it. Going over the crease, he bowled a ball wide to the boundary, and then after an unsuccessful effort to bowl a wide all along the ground, sent another round-arm ball to the ropes, thus giving away eight runs, but preventing Oxford from going in a second time. The incident gave rise to a great deal of talk and discussion, to say nothing of special articles in various newspapers. We are inclined to think, however, that in some quarters the matter was treated far too seriously, the point being overlooked that all the players immediately concerned were actuated entirely by the desire to do the best thing possible for their side. Particularly would we wish to exonerate Wells from all blame. He saw clearly that Oxford, with the idea of securing an advantage, meant to throw away a wicket, and we hold that he was perfectly justified in taking any means to prevent them that the law permitted. Whatever may be thought of the incident, it had the immediate effect of bringing the question of the follow-on under the consideration of the MCC Committee.

OXFORD v CAMBRIDGE
Lord's, July 2, 3, 4, 1896

When the MCC, yielding to the fears of some famous players, rejected a drastic alteration of law 53, and contented themselves with increasing from 80 to 120 the number of runs, involving a follow-on, it was easy to foresee that, given the same circumstances, the incident which caused so much angry discussion in the University match of 1893 would inevitably be repeated. After an interval of three years, Mr. Frank Mitchell, as captain of the Cambridge eleven, followed the example set him in 1893 by Mr. F. S. Jackson, and by palpably giving away runs to prevent his opponents from following on, forced the MCC to reconsider the whole question. Cambridge occupied nearly the whole of the first day in scoring 319. At about a quarter to four on the Friday, they were leading on the first innings by 131 runs, with only one Oxford wicket to go down. Rightly or wrongly, Mitchell judged that it would be better for his own side to go in again than to field for the rest of the afternoon, and E. B. Shine, who was then bowling at the Pavilion wicket, settled the matter by sending three balls—two of them no balls—to the boundary for four each. These twelve runs deprived Oxford of the chance of following on, and immediately afterwards the Dark Blues' innings closed for 202 or 117 behind. As they left the field, the Cambridge eleven came in for a very hostile demonstration at the hands of the public, and inside the Pavilion matters were still worse, scores of members of the MCC protesting in the most vigorous fashion against the policy that Frank Mitchell had adopted. In our opinion this display of passion was altogether illogical and uncalled for. We defended F. S. Jackson and C. M. Wells for what they did in the match of 1893, and believing that even in its amended form, law 53 is ill-adapted to modern cricket, we think Mitchell was quite entitled, in the interests of his side, to take the course he did. The incident gave rise to a long correspondence in the columns of *The Times*, and to show the difference of opinion that existed amongst the best authorities, diametrically opposite views were expressed by Lord Cobham and his younger brother, Edward Lyttelton. Lord Cobham strongly supported Mitchell's action, and Edward Lyttelton as strenuously opposed it.

Whether or not the angry demonstration they provoked, unnerved the Cambridge batsmen, we cannot say, but on going in for the second time they started very badly.

HAMPSHIRE v ESSEX
Southampton, June 24, 25, 1897

Carpenter's 73 was in every way admirably played. A curious incident happened when he had scored 67, an appeal for stumping being given against him, although neither of the bails had been removed. This fact had escaped the umpire's notice, but after some discussion, Carpenter was very properly allowed to continue his innings.

YORKSHIRE v KENT
Harrogate, July 7, 8, 1904

In this match there occurred the unprecedented instance of a game being declared void in consequence of an infringement of Law 9. It was noticed in the course of Thursday's play that the pitch at one end had broken in several places, but when on Friday morning the players turned into the field to proceed with the contest these holes had all disappeared. That the ground had been tampered with after the drawing of stumps on Thursday was agreed by the players as well as the umpires, and, exercising the powers entrusted to them, the latter ruled that the game could not stand. On the opening day Yorkshire, after dismissing Kent for 177 gained a lead of 36 runs and had three wickets in hand. Haigh on the second morning followed up some capital bowling with a fine display of batting and it was very hard luck for him that the match had to be declared void. The decision to abandon the game was come to after the conclusion of the Yorkshire innings, but, in order not to disappoint the crowd, Kent went on batting and were all out before five o'clock at which hour it had been agreed to pull up stumps. Bowling slow leg-breaks Haigh performed the 'hat trick.'

HAMPSHIRE v GLOUCESTERSHIRE
Southampton, June 27, 28, 1919

A very curious incident marked this drawn match of heavy scoring. On the second day, just at the close of Hampshire's first innings, Pothecary played a ball into the top of his pad and shook it out into the hands of Smith, the wicket-keeper. He was given out 'caught' contrary to law 33b, which states: 'if the ball, whether struck by the bat or not, lodges in the batsman's clothing, the ball shall become "dead".'

ROBERT W. CROCKETT
(1863–1935)

So many times did Crockett umpire at the end from which Blackie, the Victorian, bowled, and so many decisions did he give in favour of Blackie, that their combination gave rise to many jests. When the two met in the street, 'Rocketty' would welcome Crockett with 'How's that, Bob?' and the umpire answered with the 'out' signal, raising his hand high in the air.

WILLIAM REEVES
(1875–1944)

An admirable umpire who stood in many Test matches. In this capacity he often gave evidence of his caustic humour. Once when a batsman protested that he was not out, Reeves retorted, 'Weren't you? Wait till you see the papers in the morning.' To a bowler notorious for appealing, he remarked, 'There's only one man who appeals more than you do.' 'Oh, who's that?' asked the bowler. 'Dr Barnardo,' replied Reeves.

ALFRED ISAAC RUSSELL
(1868–1961)

For over 70 years, 50 of them as chairman, he was associated with the Deanery C.C., whom he had captained. He liked to relate how once he caught an Essex batsman behind the wicket, threw the ball into the air and loudly appealed. 'Not out,' said the umpire. 'I won't be rushed.'

FRED PRICE
(1902–1969)

Fearless as an umpire from 1950 to 1967, Price created a sensation when he three times no-balled G. A. R. Lock, the Surrey and England left-arm slow bowler, for throwing against V. S. Hazare's India touring team at The Oval. In the same season on the same ground when the Yorkshire batsmen, struggling to avoid defeat from Surrey, were being subjected to continuous barracking by the crowd, Price lay on the ground at square-leg until the noise subsided. 'I did so,' he explained afterwards, 'because three times there were catcalls just as the batsman was about to play the ball. That is not my idea of British sportsmanship and under the Laws of "fair and unfair play" I will not tolerate such things on any ground, Lord's included, where I am umpiring.'

HORACE FISHER
(1909–1974)

A left arm slow bowler for Yorkshire.

Fisher was the first bowler to register a hat-trick of lbw victims when he took five wickets for 12 runs against Somerset at Sheffield in 1932. The story has often been told that when umpire Alec Skelding having given out Mitchell-Innes and Andrews lbw, stared up the wicket at Luckes when the third appeal was made, uttered almost in disbelief, 'As God's my judge, that's out, too', and he lifted his finger.

SIDNEY BARNES
(1916–1973)

In a match in England in 1948 after a strong appeal had been turned down by A. Skelding, the umpire, a dog ran on to the field. Barnes captured the animal and carried it to Skelding with the caustic comment: 'Now all you want is a white stick.'

FRANK CHESTER
(1895–1957)

Throughout his long spell as an umpire Chester used, for counting the balls per over, six small pebbles which he picked up from his mother's garden at Bushey before he 'stood' in his first match.

UMPIRING VAGARIES
[1951]

From Frank Chester standing in the Test Match at Trent Bridge to an official acting in a club game in Australia is a far cry, but each gave a decision beyond the knowledge of regular players and followers of cricket down the ages. Chester called 'out' to an appeal for leg-before against D. J. Insole and insisted that his ruling should go on the score sheet although the ball went off the batsman's pads on to the stumps; surely this meant bowled. How Chester contrived to signal 'out' before the ball reached the stumps is difficult to realise, but, however that may be, his refusal to withdraw his verdict in favour of the more definite and satisfactory form of dismissal cannot be understood. Both for bowler and batsman 'bowled' looks far better than 'l.b.w.' in the score, and the obstinacy of such an expert as Frank Chester, regarded as the most sagacious, quickest and reliable umpire for many years, in declining to alter his attitude is more than surprising. Can it be that having given his decision he regarded the ball as 'dead' before it reached the stumps?

Umpires in Australia often come under criticism. An incident in a district game at Melbourne last October shows that clear understanding of the laws is just as necessary as practical knowledge of the game. In the case under notice Neil Harvey, the left hander, had scored 17 when a fast bowler hit the middle stump. Both bails flew into the air, but dropped into the grooves on the stumps. Harvey was on the way back to the pavilion when the umpire recalled him, saying that he was not out, his reason being that the bails must fall to the ground. Nothing in the laws makes this essential to dismissal. The bails might lodge in the wicket-keeper's pads or be caught by fieldsmen. If these suggestions seem to be stretching the point, they are mentioned to emphasise Law 31, which reads: 'The wicket shall be held to be "down" if either ball or striker's bat or person completely removes either bail from the top of the stumps,' etc.

Note to this law: 'A wicket is not "down" merely on account of disturbance of a bail, but it is "down" if a bail in falling from the wicket lodges between two of the stumps.' Surely this applied to the case in question when the 'bails flew into the air.'

ENGLAND v NEW ZEALAND
Wellington, March 24, 26, 27, 28, 1951

Midway through the innings uncertainty on the part of the umpires resulted in Moir bowling two successive overs, the last instance of which in Test cricket occurred in 1921, when Warwick Armstrong of Australia did so against England at Manchester. Moir bowled the last over before tea and the first, from the other end, afterwards.

ENGLAND v SOUTH AFRICA
Cape Town, January 1, 2, 3, 4, 5, 1957

Cricket history was made on the last day when the first handled ball dismissal occurred in a Test Match.

The 'handled ball' incident occurred when Endean pushed out his leg outside the off-stump to Laker in the second innings. The ball rose high and might well have fallen on to the stumps had not Endean thrown up a hand and diverted it. On appeal the umpire had no option but to give him out. Endean, curiously, was concerned in the previous strange Test dismissal, being the wicket-keeper when Hutton was given out 'obstructing the field' at The Oval in 1951. Endean might have made a catch had not Hutton knocked away the ball when trying to protect his wicket.

He said later: 'I thought of heading it away, but that seemed too theatrical'; it might, however, have been legal.

ENGLAND v SOUTH AFRICA
Trent Bridge, July 7, 8, 9, 11, 1960

For the first time on the tour McGlew gave of his best. He looked a class batsman again and was receiving all the help he needed when, with the stand having put on 91 in two hours, the South African captain was run out. The left-handed O'Linn played a ball from Moss to extra cover and went for a reasonably quick single. Moss dashed across the pitch to chase it and McGlew ran into his back. He stumbled and darted for the crease, but Statham had picked up and with unerring aim hit the stumps.

Cowdrey and the other England players near the broken wicket promptly appealed and Elliott, the square-leg umpire, signalled out. Elliott's decision was correct because Moss had not deliberately baulked McGlew. McGlew never hesitates when given out, but as he hastened towards the pavilion the crowd voiced their disapproval of the circumstances of his dismissal. Three times Cowdrey called to him to come back, and when he did the England captain asked the umpires if it was possible to change the verdict, but they were adamant.

LORD'S TAVERNERS v OLD ENGLAND XI
Lord's, June 16, 1962

During the afternoon session a centenarian, Joe Filliston, stood as umpire.

MCC v WEST INDIES
Lord's, May 18, 20, 21, 1963

Substitutes were required for Worrell, Allan and Gibbs. Gibbs was prevented from bowling for a time when he returned to the field and Hunte wanted to put him on immediately. The umpires considered this came under 'fair and unfair play', as he came 'warm' from the pavilion and all the other players were 'cold'. When he bowled half an hour later he soon finished the innings.

ENGLAND v WEST INDIES
The Oval, August 22, 23, 24, 26, 1963

Early on the first day after Edrich had been struck by Hall and the same bowler, in his sixth over, sent down two successive bouncers at Bolus, Buller walked over to Worrell and said, 'We don't want this sort of bowling to get out of hand otherwise I will have to speak to the bowler.'

Later, just before the close of play, Buller warned Griffith direct about his short pitched bowling in accordance with the procedure laid down in Law 46 (Fair and Unfair Play) and he also told Worrell that he had spoken to the bowler, saying 'Look this can't go on. You will have to stop it, skipper.' Griffith then remarked, 'I am allowed two every over' and Buller replied, 'No. You are not allowed any.' Happily, Worrell abided with Buller's action and after play he closed the incident, saying: 'As far as I am concerned the umpires are the sole judges of fair and unfair play.'

WEST INDIES v AUSTRALIA
Georgetown, April 14, 15, 17, 19, 20, 1965

On the eve of the match, Kippins, one of the West Indies' most experienced umpires, withdrew apparently at the insistence of the local Umpires' Association, who objected to the appointment of Jordan, of Barbados. The Association were angered because both umpires were not Guianese. The very game was threatened by this unhappy and unique situation, but it was met by appointing G. Gomez, the former Test all-rounder and now a selector, in Kippins's place. In the meantime a request was sent to Trinidad for another umpire, but although one arrived in good time, it was a tribute to Gomez's conscientious efficiency that he remained until the end. He had not previously umpired a first-class match, although he held an umpiring certificate. Gomez has been closely identified with umpiring, and an attempt to raise its standards, in the West Indies.

WESTERN AUSTRALIA v QUEENSLAND
Perth, October 30, 31, November 1, 2, 1971

Watson, believing that he had been caught in the gully by Allen off Neville, walked off the field. At the end of the day he was told by the umpire that it was not a catch; the umpire instructed the scorer to record Watson as 'retired, out'.

PAKISTAN v NEW ZEALAND
Karachi, October 30, 31, November 1, 3, 4, 1976

Frustrated by the resistance of the tail, Imran Khan unleashed three consecutive bumpers at Hadlee, who batted at number eight and umpire Shuja-ud-Din compelled Mushtaq to withdraw Imran from the attack.

WARWICKSHIRE v NORTHAMPTONSHIRE
Birmingham, May 28, 30, 31, 1977

Kanhai, in his not out 125, had the odd experience of being credited with eight runs. Three came from a leg glance chased by the wicket-keeper and five more from a penalty imposed by the Australian umpire Brooks on Steele for using a discarded wicketkeeper's glove to field the return.

DERBYSHIRE v GLAMORGAN
Chesterfield, June 10, 12, 1978

History was made just before the end of this game when Russell, fielding at short leg, was struck by a fierce blow from Nash, the ball temporarily lodging in the visor of his protective helmet. Despite this protection, Russell suffered a fractured cheekbone. The umpires had to decide whether a catch had technically been made. In the event, they ruled 'dead ball', a decision subsequently approved by the TCCB.

DERBYSHIRE v WORCESTERSHIRE
Derby, August 18, 20, 21, 1979

This game ended on an unfortunate and probably unique note of controversy. Worcestershire started their second innings at 5.50 p.m. on the last day under the impression that they had four overs in which to make 25 to win. According to the Worcestershire captain, Gifford, this information had been imparted to them by the umpires, but as the innings started a telephone call to Lord's established that the officials had apparently misinterpreted the regulations. The game was left drawn, and so Worcestershire missed the opportunity to stay in the Championship race by acquiring an extra twelve points. Gifford himself protested to Lord's and asked that the final ten minutes be replayed, a request that was turned down.

GLOUCESTERSHIRE v SOMERSET
Bristol, August 23, 25, 26, 1980

Somerset took six extra points as the team batting last in a match in which the scores finished level. Championship regulations and The Laws of Cricket were required reading at the end. Roebuck, needing a single off the last ball, attempted a run with the bails off and the ball in Brassington's gloves. But umpire Palmer had already called 'over' to finish the match after rejecting Gloucestershire's appeals for lbw.

SOUTH AUSTRALIA v VICTORIA
Adelaide, December 4, 5, 6, 7, 1980

In a low-scoring match, the turning-point occurred when, with the Victorian score at 53 for six in reply to the modest South Australian opening effort of 114, Robinson was 'caught' off the bowling of Hogg. Upon umpire Wilson indicating that he considered the bowling intimidatory, a no-ball was signalled and Robinson was recalled to the crease. The innings that followed, wherein Robinson advanced his score from 2 to 120, was instrumental in carrying Victoria to an unexpectedly easy win. Umpire Wilson was not invited to officiate in another Shield game during the season.

SHAKOOR RANA
(1936–2001)

Former Sussex captain John Barclay remembered the 1981 summer, when Shakoor Rana was umpiring in England. Barclay had been told by an Indian taxi-driver to ask 'Where's Allah?' (rather than the customary 'Howzat?') when appealing; the response would be a finger pointing to the sky. Shakoor Rana was having none of it. 'Not that silly trick again,' he said *sotto voce* as Barclay walked back to his mark.

ESSEX v MIDDLESEX
Southend, July 21, 22, 23, 1982

During the Essex first innings, Turner was twice caught by Edmonds but was allowed to bat on because umpire Oslear ruled 'no-ball', bowlers Cowans and Hughes having exceeded the one-bouncer-per-over rule. Then, in the Middlesex first innings, Downton, batting with Tomlins as his runner, was given run out while standing at the bowler's end. When Downton played the ball into the covers, both he and Tomlins raced through for a single, so contravening the law, which states that a batsman who has a runner may not himself run.

AUSTRALIA v INDIA
Melbourne, February 9, 1986

Put in, the Indians were bowled out for 187, four of their last six batsmen being run out and Amarnath being dismissed 'handled the ball' (the first instance in a one-day international) after pushing away a turning ball from Matthews that spun back towards his wicket.

GLAMORGAN v SUSSEX
Cardiff, July 2, 3, 4, 1986

Eight of the nine dismissals on the second day were for lbw and all were adjudged by Mr Julian.

ENGLAND v PAKISTAN
Perth, January 5, 1987

In Pakistan's innings a blind spot in the umpires' knowledge of the Laws cost Ramiz Raja his wicket. Not hearing umpire Crafter's no-ball call, Ramiz began walking out when he clipped Gatting to Athey at wide mid-on, whence after hesitation Athey lobbed the ball to Richards. On appeal Ramiz was given out by umpire French at square leg in contravention of Law 38(2): 'If a no-ball has been called, the striker shall not be given run out unless he attempts to run.' Rarely as such an eventuality arises, two Test umpires should have known the Law.

WORCESTERSHIRE v NORTHAMPTONSHIRE
Worcester, July 30, August 1, 2, 1988

A dispute between the captains, Neale and Cook, over whether or not Northamptonshire had been asked to follow on late on the second day, had to be settled by a TCCB ruling, which found in Worcestershire's favour. With a first-innings lead of 171, Neale insisted he had signalled to the Northamptonshire dressing-room that they should bat again. Cook was equally adamant he had not been notified, either officially or unofficially, and after taking his team into the middle, to be joined by the Worcestershire eleven, he refused to accept that his side should bat again. Umpires Bond and Harris eventually led the players off with the matter being referred to Lord's. Play for the day was finally called off at 7.25 p.m., with the official ruling that the four overs still due to be bowled should be added on to the final day. Having lost the argument, Northamptonshire succeeded in staving off defeat, Cook batting 158 minutes for a defiant 32.

OXFORD UNIVERSITY v HAMPSHIRE
Oxford, May 15, 16, 18, 1992

Umpire Holder had to withdraw because of conjunctivitis; he was replaced by Hampshire's 12th man, resting captain Mark Nicholas, and then by Oxford coach Les Lenham.

SOUTH AFRICA v INDIA
Durban, November 13, 14, 15, 16, 17, 1992

It was the first time television replays were used to settle awkward line decisions. On the second day Tendulkar changed his mind about a run and was trying to get back when Rhodes returned to Hudson. After a slight pause, Cyril Mitchley, the square-leg umpire, signalled to Karl Liebenberg, the umpire in the pavilion, by shaping a TV screen with his fingers. Thirty seconds later Liebenberg lit the green light to signify that Tendulkar was out.

SOUTH AFRICA v INDIA
Johannesburg, December 13, 1992

Television's omnipotence was further demonstrated when the Indian fielders successfully appealed for Callaghan's run-out after watching the replay on the giant screen.

SURREY v LANCASHIRE
The Oval, May 11, 1993

The TCCB used the game for the first experiment in Britain with a third umpire replaying difficult line decisions on television and communicating with his colleagues on the field by two-way radio. But Allan Jones's only involvement proved that the camera could be as uncertain as the human eye. He was unable to judge whether Wasim should be given run out, and ruled that he should stay. A photograph taken from another angle suggested that Wasim had been lucky.

ENGLAND v AUSTRALIA
Manchester, June 3, 4, 5, 6, 7, 1993

Half an hour after lunch Gooch became the fifth cricketer, and the first Englishman, to be dismissed 'handled the ball' in a Test as he instinctively flicked out with a glove at a ball dropping on to his stumps. Umpire Bird had no hesitation in giving Gooch out, with the moral victory, if not the wicket, going to Hughes for extracting extra bounce on an increasingly lifeless pitch.

BENGAL v ORISSA
Calcutta, January 5, 6, 7, 8, 1995

Kalyani was out obstructing the field. Batting with a runner, he scored a single. After it was completed his runner, D. Gandhi, was deemed to have put his hand down to pick the ball up – apparently to help the fielders – but then to have withdrawn it to attempt a second run.

SECOND ELEVEN CHAMPIONSHIP
[1996]

Still more dangerous was the batting of Somerset's Keith Parsons, who made more of an impression on the umpire than he did on the scorebook in the match against Gloucestershire at Bristol. A powerful straight drive struck Judith West, one of the country's leading women umpires, as she stood at the bowler's end, fracturing her skull and rupturing her eardrum. She said later: 'It was 6 p.m. after a hot day and I suppose my reactions were just a bit slow,' but said that she would not be retiring from the circuit.

SRI LANKA v INDIA
Colombo, August 17, 1997

There was controversy in India when TV viewers thought they saw umpire Francis wiping the ball on the Indian flag. After a spate of angry calls to newspaper offices, Francis brought out the offending cloth: a Tennent's Pilsner bar towel – with similar colours – that he had picked up in a Surrey pub.

MAHARASHTRA v TAMIL NADU
Pune, March 13, 14, 15, 16, 1999

In Tamil Nadu's second innings, George was out hit the ball twice; he blocked a ball from Hrishikesh Kanitkar then pushed it a second time. Only Kanitkar appealed and umpire M. S. S. Ranawat agreed. George, furious, gestured that he was trying to stop the ball hitting his stumps.

SRI LANKANS IN PAKISTAN, 1999–2000

Controversy dogged the final Test at Karachi as well, which Pakistan won to preserve their unbeaten record at the National Stadium. Local umpire Riazuddin had an exchange with Jayasuriya after Tillekeratne Dilshan had appeared to throw the ball at him on several occasions – an unsportsmanlike protest against decisions by Riaz which, the tourists obviously felt, deprived them of vital wickets. While no formal complaints were lodged with the referee, the Sri Lankans did make a verbal protest about Riazuddin's umpiring and referee Brian Hastings was later reported to have given him zero marks.

INDIA v ZIMBABWE
Sharjah, October 22, 2000

Friend took four wickets, including one curious dismissal when umpire Harper called wide – only for his colleague to notice that the ball had dislodged Yuvraj Singh's bail.

AUSTRALIA v INDIA
Chennai, March 18, 19, 20, 21, 22, 2001

Steve Waugh, customarily the most vigilant and calculating of bats-men, had a real lapse in concentration and became just the sixth player in 1,539 Tests to be out handled the ball. He had survived a leg before wicket appeal from Harbhajan, but as the ball bounced back towards him, he reflexively fended it away from the stumps with the palm of his right hand.

PAKISTAN v WEST INDIES
Sharjah, February 17, 2002

Ryan Hinds was outstanding at point, with the highlight his direct hit to run out the dangerous Abdul Razzaq – a dismissal momentarily in doubt when the TV umpire managed to switch on both lights at once.

ENGLAND v SRI LANKA
Manchester, July 7, 2002

Umpire Dave Orchard missed the first four overs of the match after turning up late because he thought it was a day/nighter. The third umpire, Jeremy Lloyds, stepped in.

NATIONAL VILLAGE CHAMPIONSHIP
[2002]

The North Yorkshire South final between neighbours Folkton & Flixton and Staxton had a strange conclusion. Staxton's tenth-wicket pair needed three from the last ball; the keeper appealed unsuccessfully for a stumping, then started to celebrate, assuming the ball was dead. The batsmen ran three byes, and the umpires, agreeing play was still in progress, awarded them the match.

NEW ZEALAND v SRI LANKA
Napier, April 4, 5, 6, 7, 8, 2005

Bizarrely the secret of Malinga's success – or so the New Zealanders claimed – lay in the umpires' trousers. 'We can't see him when it's a bit overcast and late in the evening,' complained Fleming on the last day. 'Last night Hamish Marshall, who's in great form, just couldn't see the ball. We asked the umpires to change the colour of their trousers. There's a period there when it gets lost in their trousers.' The umpires drew the line at changing their clothing because of Malinga's low, round-arm action and delivery from near the stumps, but on the first day they did agree to take off their dark ties and, on the last, umpire Bucknor tied a sweater round his waist as a sort of personal sightscreen.

WEST INDIES v INDIA
Kingston, May 20, 2006

There was a bizarre incident early in the West Indian innings when Sarwan pushed Pathan for a quick single. Raina's return from short midwicket hit the stumps, and the Indians appealed . . . to no one. Square-leg umpire Doctrove was on the boundary sorting out an issue with the sightscreen, and nobody had seen him go. Dead ball was called – and replays showed that Lara was just in, anyway.

Bad Luck, Bad Management

SUSSEX v HAMPSHIRE
Chichester, July 16, 17, 18, 1908

Restricted to one day's cricket which naturally led to no definite result, this match was rendered noteworthy by an altogether unpardonable course of conduct on the part of the Sussex team. Continuous rain precluded any possibility of cricket on Thursday but, although the weather continued very wet during the night, the pitch was fit for play at half-past eleven next morning. At that hour, while the Hampshire men were in attendance, only two or three members of the Sussex eleven had made their way to the Priory Park [Chichester]. Fry and Vine arrived some time later, but the majority of the side did not put in an appearance until between three and four o'clock in the afternoon. Preparations were then made for a start but the weather, always showery, turned wet again and the game was not entered upon until Saturday. Had the Sussex team arrived at the proper hour, comparatively little cricket would have been possible but that was no excuse for the non-appearance of the men. The only attempt at explanation urged was that as rain fell heavily 20 miles away, where the majority of the Sussex team stayed for the night, the cricketers concluded that no play could take place.

KENT v MIDDLESEX
Tunbridge Wells, June 15, 17, 18, 1963

The late arrival on Monday morning of nine of the Middlesex team, including Drybrough, the captain, provided a situation without parallel in the history of first-class cricket. At the close on Saturday, Middlesex, having dismissed Kent for 150, were 121 for three wickets with White 43 not out, Hooker 13 not out. The team had stayed at a local hotel on Friday night and arranged to do the same on Monday night, but they returned to their London homes at the week-end.

Three players arrived at the ground with plenty of time to spare. They were White and S. E. Russell, who had already been dismissed, and Clark, the twelfth man. White put on his pads and gloves and waited on the boundary, hoping his partner would be in time while the umpires and the Kent players went to the middle. After a wait of a liberal two minutes, the umpires led the players off the field and it was officially stated that the umpires had closed the Middlesex innings.

It was decided that Kent should begin their second innings within ten minutes and Cowdrey agreed that Clark could keep wicket while if necessary White and S. E. Russell shared the bowling, Kent providing sufficient substitute fielders to make up eleven in the field for Middlesex. Actually, Underwood, Catt, Prodger, Brown and Dye assisted their opponents, but within three overs the whole Middlesex side were present and fielding.

DERBYSHIRE v LEICESTERSHIRE
Chesterfield, September 6, 1970

Leicestershire won on run rate. Derbyshire were assured of third place, and £250 prize money, before this game began, which was probably just as well in view of its farcical conclusion. After Derbyshire had totalled 205, Leicestershire were delayed by rain at 54 for one and on the resumption needed another 99 from 13 overs, the innings having been reduced. Conditions were impossible, with rain falling and the light poor, but the umpires allowed play to continue, Tolchard taking three 6's off one over from Ward. Eventually play finished at 6.30, the umpires deciding there was not time to bowl four remaining overs; Leicestershire were ahead when scores after 23 overs were compared, but a loudspeaker announcement was necessary to inform spectators who had won.

CENTRAL DISTRICTS v PAKISTAN
New Plymouth, January 24, 1973

The game had a muddled start, Intikhab winning the toss and deciding to bat, but the Central captain M. J. F. Shrimpton being under the impression his side had been asked to bat first. So there were four batsmen padded by each side before the misunderstanding was cleared up and the game started.

SOUTH AUSTRALIA v QUEENSLAND
Adelaide, February 11, 12, 13, 14, 1977

One of the most remarkable Sheffield Shield games of all time finished in a tie – 602 runs each – from the penultimate ball of the game after Queensland had seemed assured of victory with three wickets standing and requiring four runs at the start of the last over. Carlson, Francke and Cooke were run out from the fourth, sixth and seventh balls for the tied game.

OXFORD UNIVERSITY IN 1983

One major source of annoyance in The Parks was the failure to find anyone regularly to man the scoreboard. There were occasions when it was deserted, others when it was operated by the players themselves, or by boys so small that they had to stand on crates to reach the controls. Neither the local newspaper nor the local radio station was asked to help in the search for a regular operator, which was not good enough. It should not be allowed to happen again, being a discourtesy to visiting sides and unworthy of the University's first-class status.

A SUITABLE CASE FOR COMPO

Five consecutive run-outs off the last five balls of the final over turned round the fortunes of Hatfield Town and Barnly Dun in their Doncaster and District Premier Division match on May 21, 1988. With seven balls remaining, Hatfield Town were 160 for four in reply to Barnly Dun's 166 for nine off 44 overs. Seven balls later they were all out for 164, leaving Barnly Dun the winners by 2 runs.

CUMBERLAND v LANCASHIRE
At Kendal, June 28, 29, 1989

The match was originally scheduled to be played at Carlisle but was transferred on the instructions of the TCCB because the pitch was considered unfit. It had been treated, accidentally, with weed-killer.

CLUB CRICKET SEMI-FINAL TIED THREE TIMES

In Pembrokeshire, the semi-final of The Alec Colley Cup, between Burton and Lawrenny, was tied three times before Burton gained a nine-wicket victory in the third replay on August 17, 1989. The 22-overs competition is for Second XI teams and is organised by the Pembroke County Cricket Club. In the first three matches, the scores were tied at 97, 92 and 91 respectively, with Burton batting first each time. Lawrenny were dismissed for 62 in the third replay, and Burton won with a score of 63 for one.

ZAC'S HEX COMES TO NIX
[1990]

When ten-year-old Zac Morris took five wickets in his first over for Barnsley in an Under-11 match against Derby, officials, fearing a one-sided game, stepped in and asked that Zac not bowl again. The result – Zac's team lost.

AUSTRALIA v PAKISTAN
At Sydney, February 20, 1990

O'Donnell hit out at the end, but the decisive influence on the result was Imran, who bowled a fourteen-minute maiden over in which three wickets fell. After the match, the five judges of the Man of the Match award stated publicly that they would have given it to Imran had they not been under pressure from Channel Nine to name the player before the match was over. At the time of their early decision, O'Donnell had looked like winning the game for Australia.

PAKISTANIS v BERMUDA
Bermuda, May 9, 1993

Kamran Khan, a member of a touring Philadelphian club, was one of two guest players to appear for the Pakistanis in Bermuda when their squad was reduced by injuries and contractual commitments. Nadeem Usmani, a waiter at the Southampton Princess Hotel on the island, played in the second match. Kamran was reported to have played with distinction; Nadeem, described as being more experienced as a spectator than a participant, was said to have fielded 'somewhat tentatively'.

LANCASHIRE v KENT
Lytham, August 26, 27, 28, 30, 1993

On the opening day, spectators were surprised to discover that the new paint on the seats had not quite dried, with unfortunate consequences for their dry cleaning bills.

INTERNATIONAL FLOODLIT SIXES

A floodlit six-a-side competition, involving some of the best-known international players of the past two decades, ended in farce and confusion after just one of the scheduled two days when the players' demand for immediate cash payment was not met. A crowd estimated at 'a few dozen' attended the opening day, at The Oval on September 21, 1994, to watch players such as Derek Underwood and Jeff Thomson operating a form of the game based on the successful competition in Hong Kong. The *Times* headlined its report 'Rotten enterprise worthy of contempt'.

ZIMBABWE v PAKISTAN
Harare, January 31, February 1, 2, 4, 1995

The match had a farcical start when the referee, Jackie Hendriks, demanded a second toss. Salim Malik called 'Bird', the national symbol on one side of the Zimbabwean coin, instead of 'Heads'; Andy Flower congratulated him on winning but Hendriks said he had not heard the call. Flower won at the second attempt and chose to bat.

LANCASHIRE v SUSSEX
Lytham, August 3, 4, 5, 7, 1995

The opening over on Friday was twice interrupted by snatches of Holy Communion from the nearby church of St Cuthbert, mysteriously transmitted to the public address speakers.

GLOUCESTERSHIRE v AUSTRALIANS
Bristol, May 27, 28, 29, 1997

Gloucestershire's biggest shock came after the match: the boundary rope was stolen.

OXFORD UNIVERSITY v WARWICKSHIRE
Oxford, May 18, 19, 20, 1998

With three injured men, Warwickshire needed to find an extra substitute and Darren Altree was summoned. However, after driving round for hours, he was still unable to find the ground and went home instead.

WORCESTERSHIRE v SUSSEX
Worcester, May 19, 1998

A stirring, if confusing, performance by brothers Keith and Mark Newell took Sussex to a comfortable win. They added 181 for the second wicket, but Keith had his century snatched away after it had been applauded. First, he lost two runs because an umpire's signal was amended from six to four, and then three more after a mix-up was sorted out and a scoring stroke was switched to brother Mark.

SOMERSET v HAMPSHIRE
Taunton, June 26, 27, 28, 29, 1998

No match could have lived up to the opening of this one. After three legitimate balls, bowled by McLean, the score was 17 for one. This included a single off a no-ball plus three separate wides. Under ECB regulations, these all counted for two plus any runs scored, and two of the wides evaded Aymes and crashed to the boundary, thus counting six. Then McLean found his direction and, after a dot ball, yorked Holloway.

TAMIL NADU v RAILWAYS
Chennai, February 23, 24, 25, 26, 1999

Tamil Nadu conceded 89 extras (b 43, l-b 23, n-b 23) in Railways' second innings.

NEW ZEALAND v SOUTH AFRICA
Auckland, February 27, 28, March 1, 2, 3, 1999

Several days before the first ball of this bizarre Test was bowled, it was clear that all was not well with the pitch. A fungal disease had ruined much of the grass cover and, as the third one-day international was played on a neighbouring wicket the previous weekend, there was plenty of time to examine the suspect surface. Ross Dykes, chairman of the New Zealand selectors, claimed the pitch was so poor that the teams should decamp to Hamilton, 75 miles south, but lost the argument.

However, on the first morning, the teams were surprised to see an apparently grassless, but very firm and true surface; the ground staff had applied litres of PVA glue and then rolled in grass clippings to give a healthy tinge. In what was probably a dressing-room decision, Nash, acting captain in Fleming's absence, chose to bowl after winning his first Test loss. Like most people, Nash had little idea what effect glue might have on a pitch. He might have expected a sticky dog; instead all the life went out of it.

ZIMBABWE v SRI LANKA
Harare, November 26, 27, 28, 29, 30, 1999

Seldom has a Test match had as sensational a start as this one. No bowler had previously taken a hat-trick with his first three deliveries in a Test, or as early as its second over, which is when Zoysa accomplished Sri Lanka's first hat-trick in their 95th Test. Gripper, opening in place of Rennie, padded up to a ball that nipped back, Goodwin got a faint touch to one that lifted and moved away, and finally Johnson, moving forward and across, was also given lbw by umpire Bucknor. Unfortunately, only the first two parts of the hat-trick were recorded for posterity because a power failure interrupted television coverage.

FREE STATE v BORDER
East London, September 27, 28, 29, 2002

Vasbert Drakes was recorded as timed out – only the second instance in first-class cricket – in Border's first innings: he had not even reached the ground, having been delayed on a flight from Colombo, where he had been with the West Indian squad. He did arrive in time to bowl.

INDIA v WEST INDIES
Jamshedpur, November 6, 2002

The players were called off the field after Harbhajan had conceded 17 in the 47th over. TV commentators announced that referee Mike Procter had awarded the game to West Indies under Duckworth/Lewis but, when the crowd calmed down, the game resumed and the batsmen stumbled. They needed six off the last over and three off the final ball. But an ice-cool Sarwan hit a full toss from Agarkar for four over extra cover.

VICTORIA v INDIANS
Melbourne, November 25, 26, 27, 2003

The Indians declared before the start of the second day's play, but a failure of communications meant both sides emerged to field.

ZIMBABWE v WEST INDIES
Harare, November 4, 5, 6, 7, 8, 2003

A freak incident delayed the start on the third day. As the pitch was being rolled, players were practising on the outfield; Gripper hit a ball right under the roller which left a deep indentation just short of a fast bowler's length to a left-hander. An auger was borrowed from the neighbouring golf club to replace the turf, play started one and a half hours late, and referee Gundappa Viswanath postponed lunch to allow a two-hour session.

DERBYSHIRE IN 2004

When Derbyshire changed their nickname for the 2005 League from Scorpions (the name of a lager produced by a former sponsor) to Phantoms (a vague reference to local employers Rolls-Royce), the email announcement sent via the ECB went seriously haywire, and some bemused newspapers received it 7,000 times in a day. At least the county got noticed.

WARWICKSHIRE v WORCESTERSHIRE
Birmingham, July 17, 2004

Knight was actually run out twice: the first occasion left Warwickshire 93 for three, the second (when he returned as runner for Trott) came in a final whirl of five wickets for 17.

SOMERSET v ZIMBABWEANS
Taunton, June 17, 2005

The Somerset all-rounder Keith Dutch completed an extraordinary double when he was run out at the non-striker's end backing up yet again, two days after suffering the same fate in a National League match against Scotland. Once again, it was after a deflection by the bowler, on this occasion, Streak.

YORKSHIRE v WARWICKSHIRE
Scarborough, July 19, 20, 21, 2006

It was a strange game as well as a historic one: sea mist and a distant foghorn provided an eerie atmosphere at the start, and a bizarre fault on the PA system meant spectators were given commentary on a nearby bowls match.

GLOUCESTERSHIRE v SUSSEX
Cheltenham, August 10, 11, 12 2006

In the first innings another Prior six had smashed a spectator's cornet and deposited ice cream all over his face.

GLAMORGAN v NOTTINGHAMSHIRE
Cardiff, August 30, 31, September 1, 2, 2006

Although Wales had been enjoying a dry spell, there was a damp patch at one end of the pitch, attributed to seagulls pecking holes in the tarpaulins, which an accurate seam attack exploited to dismiss Glamorgan in 48 overs.

Death and Other Indispositions

MCC AND GROUND v NOTTINGHAMSHIRE
Lord's, June 13, 14, 15, 1870

A lamentable celebrity will ever attach to this match, through the fatal accident to Summers, whose death resulted from a ball bowled by Platts in the second innings of Nottinghamshire. The wickets were excellent, and the sad mishap universally regretted.

Summers' last innings was a good one; at 12.48 he went in one wicket down with the score 29, at dinner call he had made 35 (the score 137), and at 3.30 his wicket fell to a shooter from the same hand that subsequently bowled the fatal ball. The score was 158 when Summers was out for 41 – a fact that tells how steadily and carefully he batted. This his final innings comprised eleven singles, eight 2s, three 3s, and one 5 – that 5 (a fine forward cut down to the tavern) being the last hit the poor fellow ever made, as he was then bowled by Platts; and the first ball bowled to him in the second innings was the fatal one.

JOHN PLATTS
(1848–1898)

A tragic interest attached to the start of Platts' career as a cricketer, as it was a ball bowled by him in the MCC and Notts match at Lord's in 1870 that caused the death of George Summers. At that time a very fast bowler, Platts afterwards lessened his pace and the catastrophe made such a painful impression upon him that it is said he never in subsequent years could play, with any pleasure, at Lord's ground.

MIDDLESEX v NOTTINGHAMSHIRE
Prince's, July 10, 11, 12, 1876

This match will long be remembered with a saddening interest, from its connection with the awfully sudden death of poor Tom Box, who literally died in harness, the match being in full play on the third day when Box – engaged on his duties at the score board – fell from his seat and died almost instantaneously. As a Sussex County Player; as one of the Players of England against The Gentlemen; as a South v North Cricketer; as a member of Clarke's All England Eleven; as a Ground Proprietor, and in other capacities, Box had passed a long and honourable life time on the Cricket Grounds of England, taking – and holding, for a long career – front rank as a wicket-keeper and batsman. *Scores and Biographies* tells us Box commenced cricketing when a boy. We all know he continued cricketing until he was an old man, and was 'playing his part' when Death, with such fearful suddenness, cut him down.

THE HON. IVO BLIGH'S TWELVE
IN AUSTRALIA, 1882–83

While taking part in the game called 'Tug of War' on board the *Peshawur* – the steamship which carried the English Cricketers to the Antipodes – the Hon. Ivo Bligh severely injured his right hand, and this mishap prevented his playing in either of the first six matches. This accident was not, unfortunately, the least serious one to befall a member of the team. On Monday, October 16th 1882, the *Peshawur* came into violent collision with the barque *Glenroy*, a short distance from Colombo. One of the crew, a Lascar, had one of his legs fractured in two places, but it was believed that scratches and bruises represented the full extent of the damage suffered by any one else on board. It was subsequently ascertained, however, that Morley had sustained a severe injury to one of his ribs, and though, with admirable pluck, he bowled in several matches, the unfortunate accident compelled him to leave the field during the progress of the second game, and prevented his taking any part in the 3rd, 7th, 8th, 9th, 10th, 14th, 15th, and 17th contests.

WILLIAM BATES
(1855–1900)

His career in first-class cricket – exceptionally brilliant while it lasted – was brought to a sudden and very painful close more than a dozen years back. He went out to Australia in the autumn of 1887 as a member of Mr Vernon's team, and while practising at the nets, on the Melbourne ground, met with a sad accident. Several members of the English team were on the ground at the time, and a ball hit by one of them struck Bates in the eye with such terrible force that his sight was permanently injured. Thenceforward county cricket for him was out of the question, and some little time after his return to England he attempted, in a fit of despondency, to commit suicide. He recovered his sight sufficiently to play in local matches and do some coaching, but it was of course, a painful experience for him to drop into obscurity at the age of thirty-three, after having been for over ten seasons one of the most popular cricketers in the country. Coming out in 1877, he quickly took a high position in the Yorkshire eleven, and he was still at the height of his powers when he met with his deplorable accident at Melbourne.

LANCASHIRE v GLOUCESTERSHIRE
Manchester, July 24, 25, 1884

Three-quarters of an hour's play sufficed to finish off the Lancashire innings on the Friday, and Gloucestershire went in for the second time 22 runs to the bad. They had twelve minutes' batting before luncheon, and upon resuming Dr E. M. Grace was splendidly caught at mid-off, and his brother had just succeeded him when a telegram was received announcing the death of Mrs Grace, the mother of Drs E. M. and W. G. Grace. A short consultation was held, and it was decided to at once abandon the match.

AUSTRALIANS v MIDDLESEX
Lord's, June 24, 25, 26, 1886

It must be mentioned here as a matter of record that Captain Hyde, a retired captain of the Peninsular and Oriental Company's service, died suddenly on the ground during the game. The deceased gentleman was a well-known frequenter of Lord's Ground, and his face and figure were doubtless familiar to hundreds of people.

LANCASHIRE v GLOUCESTERSHIRE
Manchester, July 21, 22, 23, 1887

Late in the afternoon a most painful incident occurred. Mr A. C. M. Croome, who was fielding at long-on, ran to try to catch a ball hit by Yates, and not noticing the railings, which at that time surrounded the enclosed portion of the ground, he came with great severity against them, and one of the points ran into his neck. He at once cried out for assistance, and was carried to the pavilion, it being for some time extremely doubtful whether or not the injury would prove fatal. Fortunately, however, the point of the railing did not enter a vital part, so after a somewhat severe illness, Mr Croome thoroughly recovered his health. The affair created a most unpleasant feeling amongst the players and the spectators, and it was at one time suggested to adjourn the game for the day, but Mr Grace wisely thought the spectators would be less anxious if the game proceeded. Immediately after the match the Lancashire committee decided to protect the points of the railings, and there is therefore little chance of a repetition of such an unusual and regrettable accident.

ESSEX v GLOUCESTERSHIRE
Leyton, August 3, 4, 5, 1899

Russell's arm was so swollen – from the effect of a mosquito bite – that he could not go in.

HARRY WILLIAM LEE
(1891–1981)

Born in Marylebone, he had a number of trials for the county between 1911 and 1914 without any notable success, but on the outbreak of war several of the amateurs on whom the county were relying joined the forces and Lee got his chance. He took it with a faultless innings of 139 against Nottinghamshire. As soon as the season was over he joined up and in May 1915 was reported killed in action. Fortunately the report was untrue: he had in fact a badly broken thigh and was a prisoner. A few months later he was repatriated with one leg shorter than the other and was told he would never play cricket again. Happily, this too proved wrong and by the summer of 1916 he was playing for MCC against schools and making runs; when first-class cricket was resumed in 1919, no-one watching him bat, bowl or, even more, chase the ball in the field would have known he had been wounded.

GLOUCESTERSHIRE v YORKSHIRE
Gloucestershire, May 7, 9, 10, 1927

Parry, an umpire whose leg had been amputated below the knee, fell in getting out of the way of a ball, and fractured the maimed limb.

WORCESTERSHIRE v WARWICKSHIRE
Worcester, August 15, 17, 18, 1931

Warwickshire, half an hour before time, defeated Worcestershire by 84 runs. Play on Saturday could not begin until one o'clock and had lasted only seventy-five minutes when rain put an end to the day's cricket. Warwickshire who had scored 52 for two wickets, resumed under strange conditions on Monday, a belt of flood water covering part of the playing field which had to be curtailed in this particular direction by some twenty-five yards. Warwickshire's innings was finished off – mainly through Brook – for 71 more runs. Parsons, discovering he had left his spectacles at home, went to fetch them, expecting his county's innings would last until after lunch and, consequent upon the collapse, he had no chance of batting.

PERCY CORRALL
(1906–1994)

'Paddy' Corrall kept wicket for the county [Leicestershire] in 285 matches from 1930 to 1951. He was barely 5ft 2in tall and in 1933 suffered one of the most frightening injuries ever seen in county cricket. Cyril Washbrook chased a ball from Ewart Astill on the leg side and hit Corrall on the head with his bat, fracturing his skull. He was on the danger list for several weeks, but not only did he pull through, he returned next season better than ever and played in every Championship match.

ESSEX v WORCESTERSHIRE
May 19, 21, 22, 1934

On Whit-Monday morning Nichol, the Worcestershire batsman, was found dead in bed – a sad event that marred the enjoyment of the match but did not prevent Worcestershire gaining first innings lead.

ESSEX v WORCESTERSHIRE
Chelmsford, May 27, 29, 30, 1939

Worcestershire had to contend with tragedy. In a car crash on Whit-Sunday evening Bull was killed and Buller injured. Defeat in such circumstances was not surprising.

SURREY HOME GUARD v SUSSEX HOME GUARD
Lord's, July 23, 1942

Abandoned. This match was given up in tragic circumstances after Andrew Ducat, the Surrey and England cricketer and international footballer, collapsed and died at the wicket. On 29, Ducat hit a ball from Eaton to mid-on. The ball was returned to the bowler, who was about to send down the next delivery when Ducat fell forward and apparently died immediately though he was moved to the pavilion and quickly taken by ambulance to a nearby hospital.

MIDDLESEX AND ESSEX v KENT AND SURREY
Lord's, August 28, 1943

Steady rain lasting many hours suggested a wet day, but after an early lunch the downfall ceased and the precaution of covering the pitch entirely enabled a start at half-past two. Meanwhile, when everyone present regarded cricket as impossible, the Arsenal club obtained permission for the brothers Compton to play at Charlton in the opening match of the football season. An injury to A. V. Avery of Essex, who tripped over his bag when leaving home for Lord's, further weakened what could be called the home team, and Arthur Fagg spent the day looking for his bag mislaid on the railway.

WORCESTERSHIRE v YORKSHIRE
Worcester, June 3, 5, 6, 1961

Spectators at this casualty-stricken match will long remember the plucky effort of Don Wilson. The end of Yorkshire's unbeaten record in the championship looked imminent when nine wickets tumbled to a combination of pace and spin with 36 runs still required. Then Wilson, with his left arm in plaster from the elbow to the knuckles because of a fractured thumb, joined Platt with twenty-five minutes to play. Though the pain quickly prompted him to bat one-handed, Wilson swept Gifford twice for 4 and when Flavell took the new ball five minutes from the end with 22 runs still needed, he immediately struck three boundaries and a two with one-handed drives. This over also brought four byes. Then Platt took a single off Coldwell and the crowd rose to cheer when Wilson straight drove to the boundary to complete a thrilling finish. He hit 29 in a last-wicket stand of 37.

WEST INDIES v ENGLAND
Bridgetown, March 13,.14, 15, 17, 18, 1981

Though put in on a pitch which was at its liveliest on the first morning, West Indies dominated a match tragically marred by the death, after play on the second evening, of Ken Barrington, assistant-manager and coach of the England team.

With a first innings lead of 143, the loss of Greenidge before the end of the second day scarcely troubled West Indies, and they batted comfortably if cautiously through the third day, which England played with heavy hearts after Ken Barrington's death in the night. The two teams, officials and a capacity crowd of 15,000 stood in silence in his memory before play began.

SOMERSET v WORCESTERSHIRE
Weston-super-Mare, August 12, 13, 14, 1981

With the pitch at its most unpleasant, Roebuck retired with a damaged finger and three batsmen were laid low by blows to the groin.

A FINE TRIBUTE

'I can't think of any group with whom my husband would rather have spent his last hours.' Mrs Percy Norris, widow of the British Deputy High Commissioner, speaking after the assassination in Bombay of her husband a few hours after he had hosted a reception to the England cricket team in November 1984.

LANCASHIRE v DERBYSHIRE
Manchester, June 27, 29, 30, 1987

Stanworth badly bruised his hand when a door shut on it on the morning of the second day, so Fowler kept wicket for the remainder of the first innings and Hughes took over in the second.

SRI LANKA A v ENGLAND A
Colombo, March 1, 2, 3, 4, 5, 1991

Play had originally been scheduled for March 6, with March 4 set aside as the rest day, but this was rearranged when March 6 was declared a national day of mourning following the assassination of Sri Lanka's State Minister for Defence on March 2.

SURREY v DERBYSHIRE
The Oval, May 30, 31, June 1, 3, 1996

Thorpe made 185, Butcher scored fifties in both innings, and Stewart was within touching distance of joining him but had to retire before the final day's play because his wife had gone into hospital. This was considered an 'unavoidable cause' for retirement under Law 2.9, and he was ruled not out. Wells was too badly hurt to hobble back to the pavilion at tea on the final day, so ground staff took a deckchair and a cup of tea to the middle for him, and Cork stayed to keep him company.

BRIGHTON COLLEGE IN 1996

The side included twins, Chris and James Sell, who each dislocated a shoulder in the same match – against the Old Brightonians.

EUROPEAN NATIONS CUP
[1997]

France retained the Nations Cup at Zuoz, Switzerland, in astonishing circumstances. They beat Germany by one run in a pulsating 50-over final. The unwitting hero was France's last man, David Bordes, who was hit on the forehead, and staggered through for a single at the end of the French innings before collapsing with a fractured skull. With two balls left, Germany, chasing 267, were 260 for nine: a top-edge fumbled by third man plopped over the rope for six. The Germans completed the two runs they needed for victory while the last ball was still skying to mid-on, where Valentin Brumant eventually caught it. So the Bordes head-bye proved a match-winner. He had to spend the next two weeks

in hospital, and was ill for some time but, happily, was able to resume playing indoor cricket before Christmas. Bordes normally bats with a helmet but did not bother this time because he had only the one ball to face.

LEEWARD ISLANDS v WINDWARD ISLANDS
Philipsbury, February 6, 7, 8, 9, 2004

The 34-year-old former Test batsman Stuart Williams had the little finger on his right hand amputated after it was broken in the field, and gangrene set in. The Players' Association took up Williams's case on the grounds that he had received questionable medical attention.

SOMERSET v SURREY
Taunton, May 1, 2005

Ramprakash, after dislocating his toe on the pavilion steps fetching a cup of tea, batted at No. 7 and scored 11.

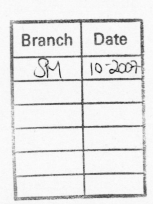

Branch	Date
SM	10-2007